PRESENTED TO:

The strength of our hope is the strength of our prayer.

Carlo Carretto

PRESENTED BY:

Life's Daily Prayer Book

ISBN: 1-404-18513-5

The quoted ideas expressed in this book (but not Scripture verses) are not, in all cases, exact quotations, as some have been edited for clarity and brevity. In all cases, the author has attempted to maintain the speaker's original intent. In some cases, quoted material for this book was obtained from secondary sources, primarily print media. While every effort has been made to ensure the accuracy of these sources, the accuracy cannot be guaranteed. For additions, deletions, corrections or clarifications in future editions of this text, please write ELM HILL BOOKS.

Manuscript written by Vicki J. Kuyper in conjunction with Snapdragon Editorial Group, Inc.

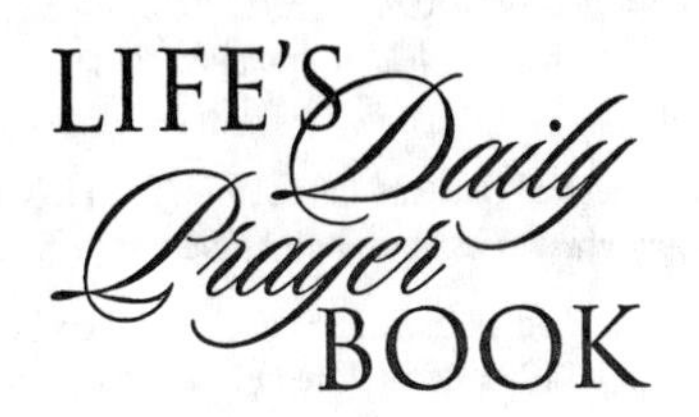

Prayers to Encourage and Comfort the Soul

Elm Hill Books
An Imprint of J. Countryman®

An old hymn goes: "What a friend we have in Jesus, all our sins and griefs to bear. What a privilege to carry everything to God in prayer." Wonderful words, aren't they? Comforting, strengthening, liberating words of truth! In the Bible, God invites us to friendship with Him, a friendship that urges us to cast all our cares on Him.

Life's Daily Prayer Book was designed to guide and inspire you as you reach out to God in friendship and converse with Him concerning the issues, activities, and relationships that define your life. Think of these written prayers as letters to your best friend—God. Make them your own by adding the names of family and friends and specific needs. And don't forget to record and date your answers. May God bless you as you embark on this exciting adventure in prayer.

Life's Daily Prayer Book

Prayers to Encourage and Comfort the Soul

Prayer is the peace of our spirit,
The stillness of our thoughts,
The evenness of our recollection,
The sea of our meditation,
The rest of our cares,
And the calm of our tempest.

Jeremy Taylor

Daily Prayers …

Daily prayer for ...

salvation

Jesus Christ from Nazareth, the man you crucified, but whom God raised from the dead. There is salvation in no one else!

Acts 4:10, 12 NLT

Dear Heavenly Father:

I've tried to live my life by my own rules, turning my back on You and Your love for too long. Please forgive me for each and every one of my offenses. I know they're responsible for Your Son's death on the cross.

I know that Jesus' death was not only a sacrifice but also a gift—a gift of absolute forgiveness and eternal salvation. I want to accept that gift with open arms and an open, repentant heart. I long to learn to love You as much as You love me. I want to know what it's like to call You "Lord" and really mean it.

Show me how to put my life in Your hands.

Amen.

You have been saved by grace because you believe. You did not save yourselves. It was a gift from God.

Ephesians 2:8 NCV

MY PERSONAL PRAYER

Salvation comes through a cross and a crucified Christ.
Andrew Murray

Dear Father:

Amen

With joy you will draw water from the wells of salvation
Isaiah 12:3 NRSV

The wages of sin is death, but the gift of God is eternal life in Christ Jesus our Lord
Romans 6:23 NKJV

Daily prayer for ... *peace*

Tell God what you need, and thank him for all he has done. If you do this, you will experience God's peace, which is far more wonderful than the human mind can understand.

Philippians 4:6, 7 NLT

Dear Heavenly Father,

You are the source of peace in any and every circumstance. Though from the outside, my life seems anything but peaceful, I know that You are my eye of the storm. You calm my heart, quiet my mind, and help bring my emotions into line with the truth—You are in control.

One by one, I put my worries and concerns into Your mighty hands, assured that You know exactly what to do with each one of them. Help me to cling more tightly to You than to my problems. I want to know the peace that comes only from drawing close to Your side, minute by minute, day by day.

Amen.

You, Lord, give true peace. You give peace to those who depend on You. You give peace to those who trust You.

Isaiah 26:3 NCV

MY PERSONAL PRAYER

Peace reigns where our Lord reigns.
Julian of Norwich

Dear Father:

Amen

Let the peace of God rule in your hearts.
Colossians 3:15 NKJV

Jesus said, "I am leaving you with a gift— peace of mind and heart."
John 14:27 NLT

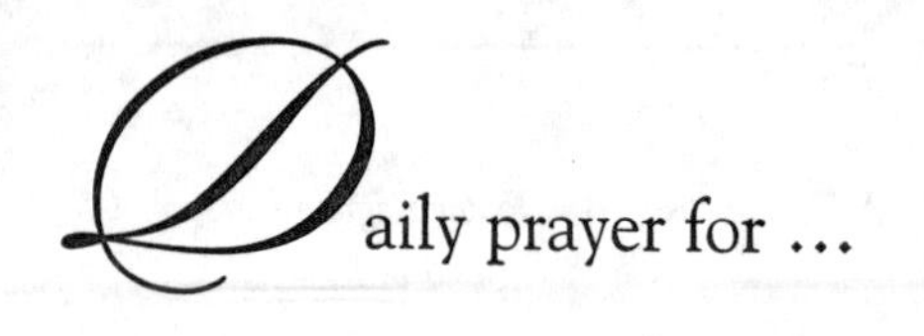

Daily prayer for ...

wisdom

If you need wisdom—if you want to know what God wants you to do—ask him, and he will gladly tell you.

James 1:5 NLT

Dear Heavenly Father,

You are a God of wisdom who loves it when Your children follow in Your footsteps. Show me how to walk in Your ways, how to relate to others wisely and well, how to apply what You teach me to my daily life.

I need Your wisdom guiding me every step of the way. Your wisdom is so different from the way I naturally think. You've said that I have to lose my life to save it, that I need to store up treasure in heaven instead of on earth, and that I am at my greatest when I become a servant. Help me lean on Your wisdom for guidance, rather than following the wisdom of this world.

Amen.

The wisdom that comes from heaven is first of all pure. It is also peace loving, gentle at all times, and willing to yield to others. It is full of mercy and good deeds. It shows no partiality and is always sincere.

James 3:17 NLT

MY PERSONAL PRAYER

Men may acquire knowledge, but wisdom is a gift direct from God.

Bob Jones

Dear Father:

Amen

Wisdom begins with respect for the Lord.

Psalm 111:10 NCV

The foolishness of God is wiser than men, and the weakness of God is stronger than men.

1 Corinthians 1:25 NKJV

Daily prayer for …

joy

Be joyful always; pray continually; give thanks in all circumstances, for this is God's will for you in Christ Jesus.

1 Thessalonians 5:16–18 NIV

Dear Heavenly Father,

My heart is filled with Your joy, a joy that goes so much deeper than happiness and has nothing to do with the circumstances I find myself in at the moment. It's a joy born of the awareness of Your continual presence and love in my life. And it's filling my heart to overflowing with gratitude.

Even when the emotions that joy often brings seem far away, show me how to nurture a joyful attitude, a heart that constantly delights in simply being Your child. May the joy You've poured into my life refresh the lives of those around me in a way that points straight back to You.

Amen.

The joy of the LORD is your strength.

Nehemiah 8:10 NRSV

MY PERSONAL PRAYER

Sheer joy is God's, and this demands companionship.

Thomas Aquinas

Dear Father:

____

____

____

____

____

____

____

Amen

Jesus said, "Ask and you will receive, and your joy will be complete."

John 16:24 NIV

Rejoice in the Lord always. Again I will say, rejoice!

Philippians 4:4 NKJV

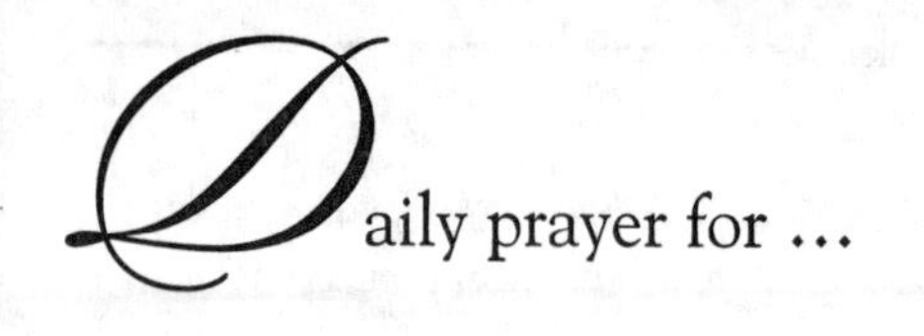

Daily prayer for ... *comfort*

The LORD is close to the brokenhearted and saves those who are crushed in spirit.

Psalm 34:18 NIV

Dear Heavenly Father,

Your Word says that You are "the God of all comfort." I desperately need that comfort right now. Please hold me close and console my heart in a way that not even my closest friends ever could.

I know that because You love me, You feel my pain as though it were Your own. You understand every ache, every question, every tear. My only hope of true healing is found in You and Your power. I'm relying on that hope this moment. I'm turning to You as a child turns to a parent, with arms outstretched and a simple heartfelt plea for "help." Be my comfort, right here, right now.

Amen.

The Father is a merciful God, who always gives us comfort. He comforts us when we are in trouble, so that we can share the same comfort with others in trouble.

2 Corinthians 1:3, 4 CEV

MY PERSONAL PRAYER

Higher comfort there cannot be than to rest in the Father's heart.
Andrew Murray

Dear Father:

Amen

Whenever I am anxious and worried, you comfort me and make me glad.
Psalm 94:19 GNT

Jesus said, "Blessed are those who mourn, for they will be comforted."
Matthew 5:4 NIV

Daily prayer for ...

power

With God's power working in us, God can do much, much more than anything we can ask or think of.

Ephesians 3:20 NCV

Dear Heavenly Father,

Challenges lie ahead that I could never handle on my own. But I know that I'm not alone. You are here working through me. Let Your Spirit fill me with the power I need to accomplish what You've asked me to do.

As I lean on You, let Your power become evident to others. Let them see the miracle of Your hand working in the world—and in my life.

Take the strengths and abilities You've already given me and show me how to put them to good use. Then take my weaknesses and work through them as well, in a way that brings true glory to Your precious name.

Amen.

We are like clay jars in which this treasure is stored. The real power comes from God and not from us.

2 Corinthians 4:7 CEV

MY PERSONAL PRAYER

The Kingdom of God is simply God's power enthroned in our hearts.
John Main

Dear Father:

____

____

____

____

____

____

____

Amen

The prayer of a godly person is powerful.
It makes things happen.
James 5:16 NIrV

You will receive power when the Holy Spirit comes on you.
Acts 1:8 NIV

Daily prayer for ...

forgiveness

If we confess our sins to him, he is faithful and just to forgive us and to cleanse us from every wrong.

1 John 1:9 NLT

Dear Heavenly Father,

I look at You and see perfection. I look at myself and see a work in progress. I know Your Spirit is at work within me, but sometimes I feel as though I'm moving backward rather than forward. I'm going back over ground that I should have long ago conquered.

But You know my heart. You know how much I long to be the person You created me to be. I'm so sorry for falling back into patterns of the "old" me. Please make me new again. Give me a fresh start. Cover me once again with Your "amazing grace" and forgive me.

Amen.

Forgive as quickly and completely as the Master forgave you.

Colossians 3:13 MSG

MY PERSONAL PRAYER

Forgiveness means the refusal on God's part to let our guilty past affect His relationship with us.
Author Unknown

Dear Father:

Amen

All who have faith in Jesus will have their sins forgiven in his name.
Acts 10:43 CEV

You are a God of forgiveness, always ready to pardon, gracious and merciful, slow to become angry, and full of love and mercy.
Nehemiah 9:17 TLB

Daily prayer for ... *protection*

You are my hiding place; you will protect me from trouble and surround me with songs of deliverance.

Psalm 32:7 NIV

Dear Heavenly Father,

I am so vulnerable in this world, physically, emotionally, and spiritually. My only true protection comes from You. You know when a sparrow falls from the sky and when I am in for a fall of my own. Please be my safety net today.

Guard my heart with Your Word. Help me to be wise about the places I go and the things I do. And when I've done everything I can to walk the right path, let me rest, knowing that my safety and the safety of those I love ultimately depends on You.

I know that no matter what happens, You will not only be my strength but my shield.

Amen.

God will cover you with his wings; you will be safe in his care; his faithfulness will protect and defend you.

Psalm 91:4 GNT

MY PERSONAL PRAYER

Prayer is that mightiest of all weapons that created natures can wield.

Martin Luther

Dear Father:

Amen

God guards the course of the just and protects the way of his faithful ones.

Proverbs 2:8 NIV

Whoever trusts in the LORD shall be safe.

Proverbs 29:25 NKJV

Daily prayer for ...

courage

Be strong and courageous. Do not be terrified;
do not be discouraged, for the LORD your
God will be with you wherever you go.
Joshua 1:9 NIV

Dear Heavenly Father,

Calm my quaking heart. Right now, I'd rather turn and run from the circumstances ahead. But I know that's not what You want me to do. So I'm trusting in You to give me the strength to move forward, to face my fears with the supernatural courage that I know comes from Your throne and not my own unsettled emotions.

Please help me hold my head high and do the right thing. Help me care less about what others have to say and more about what You would have me do. Give me the courage I need when I need it most.

Amen.

God's Spirit doesn't make cowards out of us.
The Spirit gives us power, love, and self-control.
2 Timothy 1:7 CEV

MY PERSONAL PRAYER

Courage is not the absence of fear,
but the judgment that something
else is more important than fear.
Ambrose Redmoon

Dear Father:

Amen

Stay brave and strong. Show love in everything you do.
1 Corinthians 16:13, 14 CEV

Jesus said, "In this world you will have trouble.
But take heart! I have overcome the world."
John 16:33 NIV

Daily prayer for ...

strength

Those who trust in the LORD for help will find their strength renewed.

Isaiah 40:31 GNT

Dear Heavenly Father,

I feel so weak and powerless. But I know that when my own strength has reached its limit, You invite me to lean on You.

Lord, You are not my crutch, enabling me to limp through life. You are my fortress. You help me stand up to any attack that comes my way. You provide me with a safe place to renew my strength when my perseverance is put to the test. You strengthen me physically and emotionally when life is pushing hard from every direction.

Please be my fortress right now. Give me the strength to face whatever today brings my way.

Amen.

I ask the Father in his great glory to give you the power to be strong through his Spirit.

Ephesians 3:16 NCV

MY PERSONAL PRAYER

Anxiety does not empty tomorrow of its sorrows, but today of its strength.

Charles Haddon Spurgeon

Dear Father:

____

____

____

____

____

____

____

Amen

It is God who arms me with strength and makes my way perfect.

2 Samuel 22:33 NIV

Be strong in the Lord and in the power of His might.

Ephesians 6:10 NKJV

Daily prayer for ...

rest

Jesus said, "Take my yoke and put it on you, and learn from me, because I am gentle and humble in spirit; and you will find rest."

Matthew 11:29 GNT

Dear Heavenly Father,

Right now my schedule has no time for rest, but my body needs it, my mind longs for it, and my spirit craves it. Renew me, inside and out.

For just a moment, I am stopping to rest in You. Be my mountain hideaway, my sandy island shore, my hammock in the sun. Help me take each of the concerns and demands that are taking such a toll on my life and place them in Your hands—hands that are big enough to hold them all. Hands that cup around my face with a Father's tender love. Hands that made the world—and me.

Calm my spirit with the quiet assurance of Your presence. Teach me how to rest in You.

Amen.

There is a special rest still waiting for the people of God. For all who enter God's rest will find rest from their labors.

Hebrews 4:9, 10 NLT

MY PERSONAL PRAYER

You have created us for yourself,
and our hearts cannot be stilled
until they find rest in you.
Saint Augustine of Hippo

Dear Father:

Amen

Rest in the LORD, and wait patiently for Him.
Psalm 37:7 NKJV

The LORD says, "Stop right where you are! Look for the old, godly way, and walk in it. Travel its path, and you will find rest for your souls."
Jeremiah 6:16 NLT

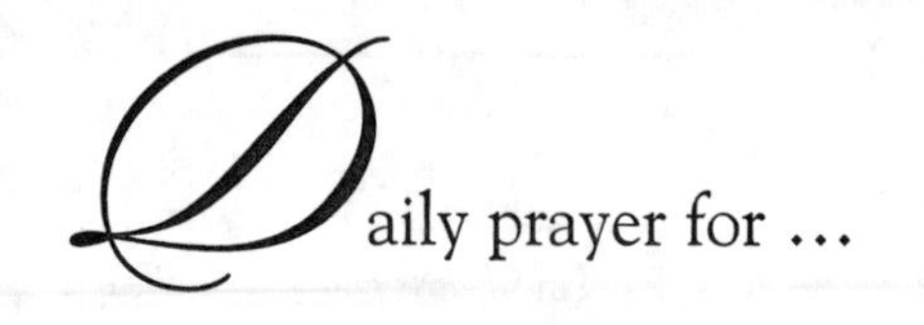

Daily prayer for …

hope

The Scriptures were written to teach and encourage us by giving us hope.
Romans 15:4 CEV

Dear Heavenly Father,

Please replace my discouragement with hope. Bring to mind truths from Your Word that I can cling to—promises that will never fail, hope that is found in knowing that You love me eternally and without reservation. Remind me of these important things: You will supply all my needs; You will never leave me nor will You forsake me; You keep track of every tear I cry, for You are close to the brokenhearted.

You are the only source of hope that will never fail. Show me how to take what I know about You in my mind and let it take root in my heart, creating a victory garden of hope to encourage me when I need it most.

Amen.

God has great mercy, and because of his mercy he gave us a new life. He gave us a living hope because Jesus Christ rose from death.
1 Peter 1:3 NCV

MY PERSONAL PRAYER

Hope is faith holding out its hand in the dark.

George Iles

Dear Father:

Amen

The LORD's delight is in those who honor him,
those who put their hope in his unfailing love.
Psalm 147:11 NLT

The mystery is that Christ lives in you,
and he is your hope of sharing in God's glory.
Colossians 1:27 CEV

Daily prayer for ...

patience

I wait for the LORD, my soul waits,
and in His word I do hope.
Psalm 130:5 NKJV

Dear Heavenly Father,

My patience is wearing thin. You know I want things to run on my schedule. Even so, I know that waiting for Your timing is the right thing to do. Show me how to watch while I wait, to grow as my patience is put to the test.

Open my eyes to what You want to teach me while I'm waiting. Stretch my patience in a way that enlarges my love for others, as well as for You. Show me how to wait well, to tame my impulsiveness, and to let go of my desire to control what's going on around me. Remind me that You have everything under control.

Amen.

If we look forward to something we don't have yet,
we must wait patiently and confidently.
Romans 8:25 NLT

MY PERSONAL PRAYER

There are three answers to prayer:
yes, no, and wait.
Author Unknown

Dear Father:

____

____

____

____

____

____

____

Amen

A man's wisdom makes him patient.
Proverbs 19:11 NIrV

Always be humble and patient.
Ephesians 4:2 NCV

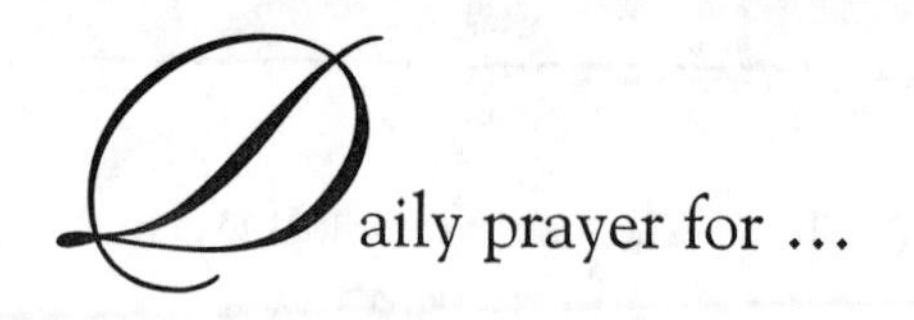

Daily prayer for ...

contentment

Having food and clothing,
with these we shall be content.
1 Timothy 6:8 NKJV

Dear Heavenly Father,

No matter how much You bless me, there's always that nagging ache for just a little more. Please break me of the habit of comparison, measuring what I have against what others have. Help me focus on all You've given me—blessings and gifts that transcend earthly possessions. You've been so generous to me in so many ways. Help me recognize each gift with a heart filled with gratitude.

And, Lord, even if the day comes when I feel I have nothing at all, I will be content knowing that I have You in my life and that I am the recipient of Your incomparable love and grace.

Amen.

I have learned to be satisfied with what I have. ... I am content, whether I am full or hungry, whether I have too much or too little.
Philippians 4:11, 12 GNT

MY PERSONAL PRAYER

The heart is rich when it is content,
and it is always content when its
desires are fixed on God.
Miguel Febres Cordero–Munzo

Dear Father:

Amen

God satisfies the longing soul,
and fills the hungry soul with goodness.
Psalm 107:9 NKJV

A good man will be satisfied from above.
Proverbs 14:14 NKJV

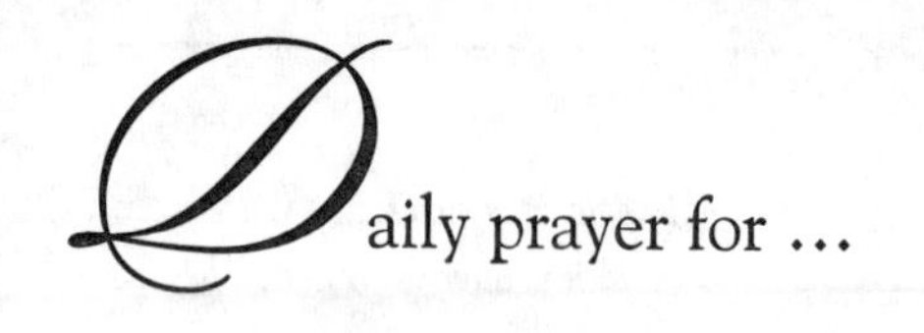

Daily prayer for ...

faith

Jesus said, "I assure you, even if you had faith as small as a mustard seed you could say to this mountain, 'Move from here to there,' and it would move. Nothing would be impossible."

Matthew 17:20 NLT

Dear Heavenly Father,

I know the only way to watch my faith grow is to put it to the test. I'm asking You to do that now. That's not an easy prayer to pray. It makes me a little nervous, a little apprehensive about what may lie ahead. But my desire for my faith to grow is stronger than my fear about what it will take to make that happen.

I can relate to the father who, out of concern for his ailing son, turned to Jesus and said, "I do believe; help me overcome my unbelief!" Help me in the same way that Jesus helped that earnestly seeking father. Please strengthen my faith.

Amen.

What if I had faith that moved mountains?
I would be nothing, unless I loved others.

1 Corinthians 13:2 CEV

MY PERSONAL PRAYER

Faith is the daring of the soul to go farther than it can see.
William Newton Clarke

Dear Father:

____

____

____

____

____

____

____

Amen

Fight the good fight of the faith, take hold of the eternal life, to which you were called.
1 Timothy 6:12 NCV

Faith comes from listening to this message of good news—the Good News about Christ.
Romans 10:17 NLT

Daily prayer for ...

perseverance

Blessed is the man who keeps on going when times are hard.

James 1:12 NIrV

Dear Heavenly Father,

Sometimes life feels like a mountain with an unreachable summit. I climb and climb, and keep thinking the end is just around the next bend in the trail. But, instead, I find another rugged peak I have to scale.

I want to give life all I've got to make the most of all You've given me, but I'm tired and often discouraged. Please help me put one foot in front of the other and keep moving forward. Help me persevere until the end—not with a sense of drudgery and duty but with an energizing fire of joy and purpose.

Amen.

I'm staying on your trail; I'm putting one foot in front of the other. I'm not giving up.

Psalm 17:5 MSG

MY PERSONAL PRAYER

Perseverance is not a long race;
it is many short races one after
another.

Walter Elliott

Dear Father:

Amen

Patient endurance is what you need now, so you will continue to do God's will. Then you will receive all that he has promised.

Hebrews 10:36 NLT

Let us run with endurance the race that is set before us.

Hebrews 12:1 NKJV

Daily prayer for ...

purpose

Pray that our God will make you fit for what he's called you to be.
2 Thessalonians 1:11 MSG

Dear Heavenly Father,

I want my life to count. I know that in Your eyes it always has—and it always will. But I want to reach my true potential and become the person You created me to be.

Give me a glimpse of myself through Your eyes. Show me how I can best put my unique gifts, circumstances, and relationship with You to use in ways that will make a positive difference in this world.

Guide my decisions and direction in ways that best suit Your purposes, and not my own personal dreams. I want Your dreams for my life to become my own. Please use me as only You can.

Amen.

We are God's masterpiece. He has created us anew in Christ Jesus, so that we can do the good things he planned for us long ago.
Ephesians 2:10 NLT

MY PERSONAL PRAYER

God sees every one of us;
He creates every soul—
for a purpose.
John Henry Newman

Dear Father:

Amen

Watch your step. Use your head. Make the most of every chance you get. These are desperate times!
Ephesians 5:15, 16 MSG

Our only goal is to please God.
2 Corinthians 5:9 NCV

Daily prayer for ...
my spouse

A man leaves father and mother, and in marriage,
he becomes one flesh with a woman—no longer
two individuals, but forming a new unity.

Mark 10:7, 8 MSG

Dear Heavenly Father,

After You created the universe and all of the incredible creatures of this world, You declared that everything You had made was "good." The only thing You declared "not good," was "to be alone."

Thank You for the gift of marriage, for teaching my spouse and me what love really means by helping us work through a lifelong relationship. I pray that You would draw my spouse even closer to You. Show me how to be a loving support and encourager, helping my spouse to better reflect Your image in every aspect of life.

Together, help us deal with the small things before they become big ones—and tackle the big things with courage, compassion, and commitment.

Amen.

Pray for each other so that you can live together whole and healed.

James 5:16 MSG

MY PERSONAL PRAYER

Success in marriage does not come merely through finding the right mate, but through being the right mate.

Barnett Brickner

Dear Father:

Amen

Give honor to marriage,
and remain faithful to one another in marriage.
Hebrews 13:4 NLT

Find a good spouse, you find a good life—
and even more: the favor of GOD!
Proverbs 18:22 MSG

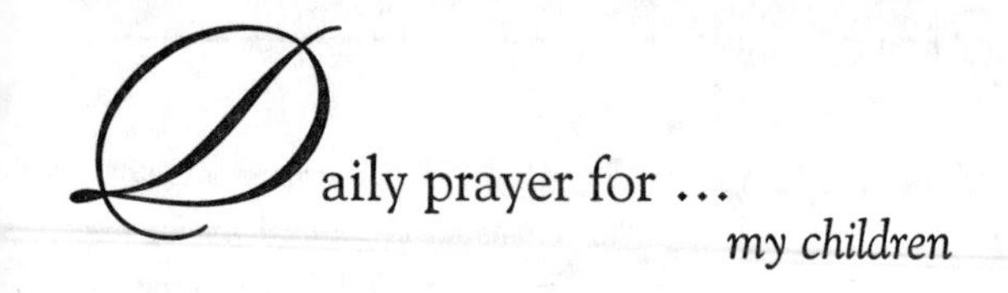

Daily prayer for … *my children*

God-loyal people, living honest lives, make it much easier for their children.
Proverbs 20:7 MSG

Dear Heavenly Father,

My children are not mine alone. They're also Yours. Help me rest in this truth and do all I can to make sure that my children know how to rest in it as well.

Each day, help my children to mature into the people You created them to be. Lead them on their own separate paths, even if they are different from the ones I envision for them. Give me wisdom to know how to walk beside them along this road, as far as You would have me go.

Keep my children safe in Your powerful, yet tender, embrace. You know how much they mean to me. Help me show that love to them in a tangible way.

Amen.

Children are a gift from the LORD; They are a real blessing.
Psalm 127:3 GNT

MY PERSONAL PRAYER

If you can give your children a trust in God, they will have one sure way of meeting all the uncertainties of existence.

Eleanor Roosevelt

Dear Father:

____

____

____

____

____

____

____

Amen

Oh, how blessed are you parents, with your quivers full of children!

Psalm 127:5 MSG

Jesus said, "Let the children come to me. Don't stop them! For the Kingdom of God belongs to such as these."

Mark 10:14 NLT

Daily prayer for ...

my siblings

God places the lonely in families.
Psalm 68:6 NLT

Dear Heavenly Father,

Thank You for the siblings You've placed in my life. Thank You for the memories we've made together, the good as well as the bad. Everything we've gone through as a family has helped to open my eyes to the joys and challenges of unconditional love. In turn, that's given me a better understanding of Your perfect love.

Please bless my siblings right now. Meet their needs spiritually as well as physically. Help our love for each other to grow until it resembles Your own. Make Your presence known in each of our lives in ways that our individual hearts long for most.

Amen.

Whoever does not provide for relatives, especially for family members, has denied the faith and is worse than an unbeliever.
1 Timothy 5:8 NRSV

MY PERSONAL PRAYER

When we are linked by the power of prayer, we, as it were, hold each other's hand as we walk side by side along a slippery path.

Gregory the Great

Dear Father:

Amen

Pray every way you know how, for everyone you know.

1 Timothy 2:1 MSG

Jesus said, "Whoever does the will of God is My brother and My sister and mother."

Mark 3:35 NKJV

Daily prayer for ...

my parents

This is the promise: If you honor your father and mother, "you will live a long life, full of blessing."

Ephesians 6:3 NLT

Dear Heavenly Father,

Although I'm an adult, my parents still hold an important place in my life. Help me show them love and respect in ways that honor You as I honor them. As they get older, show me how to care for them in practical ways. Take the words we speak to each other and help us communicate on a deeper and more honest level, a level that will nurture real friendship.

Thank You for making us family. In spite of all of our faults and weaknesses, continue to teach us what love really means by drawing us closer.

Amen.

Listen with respect to the father who raised you; and when your mother grows old, don't neglect her.

Proverbs 23:22 MSG

MY PERSONAL PRAYER

Honor your parents both in your thoughts, and speech, and behavior.

Richard Baxter

Dear Father:

____

____

____

____

____

____

____

Amen

Make your father happy! Make your mother proud!

Proverbs 23:25 MSG

Show respect to the aged, honor the presence of an elder, fear your God.

Leviticus 19:32 MSG

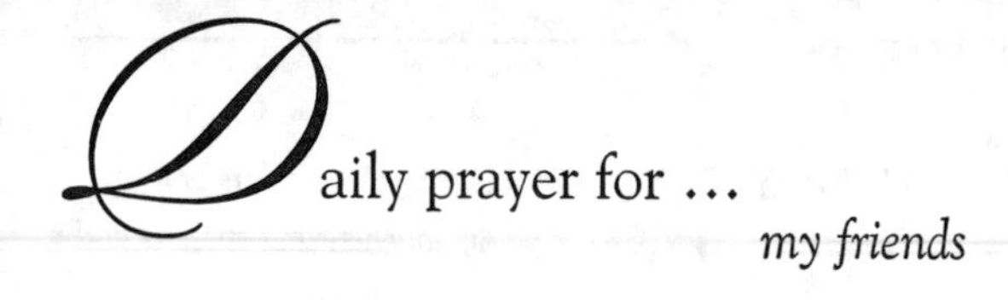

Daily prayer for … *my friends*

Every time I think of you, I give thanks to my God. I always pray for you, and I make my requests with a heart full of joy.

Philippians 1:3, 4 NLT

Dear Heavenly Father,

Just seeing the face of a friend, hearing a familiar voice—even receiving an envelope with the return address of someone who's close to my heart while distant in terms of miles—fills me with thankfulness. Lord, You have blessed me with amazing friends. Thank You for each and every one, for the unique way You created them and for the memories we've made over the years.

Work in the lives of my friends today. Teach me how to be a better friend to each of them, helping them learn more about Your love through me.

Amen.

Two are better than one, because they have a good reward for their labor. For if they fall, one will lift up his companion.

Ecclesiastes 4:9, 10 NKJV

MY PERSONAL PRAYER

Friendship that flows from the heart cannot be frozen by adversity, as the water that flows from the spring cannot congeal in winter.

James Fenimore Cooper

Dear Father:

____

____

____

____

____

____

____

Amen

Reliable friends who do what they say are like cool drinks in sweltering heat—refreshing!

Proverbs 25:13 MSG

Friends come and friends go, but a true friend sticks by you like family.

Proverbs 18:24 MSG

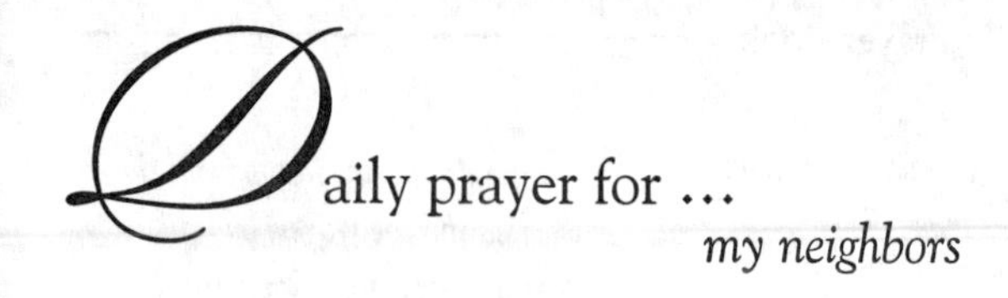

Daily prayer for ...
my neighbors

Jesus said, "Love your neighbor as you love yourself."
Matthew 19:19 NCV

Dear Heavenly Father,

You've not only placed me in a family but also in a neighborhood of potential friends. You have given me a place to live, as well as a purpose in that place. The trouble is that I often get so busy that I forget about those who live just down the street and just around the corner.

Give me a passion to make a difference in the lives of my neighbors, Lord. Help me to respond to Your urging to learn not only their names but also their needs. Then help me to reach out to help, listen, and share Your Word and my life with each one.

Amen.

If you can help your neighbor now, don't say, "Come back tomorrow, and then I'll help you."
Proverbs 3:28 NLT

MY PERSONAL PRAYER

If you want your neighbor to know what Christ will do for him, let the neighbor see what Christ has done for you.

Author Unknown

Dear Father:

Amen

Do not covet your neighbor's house or land… or anything else your neighbor owns.

Deuteronomy 5:21 NLT

Don't talk about your neighbors behind their backs— no slander or gossip, please.

Proverbs 24:28 MSG

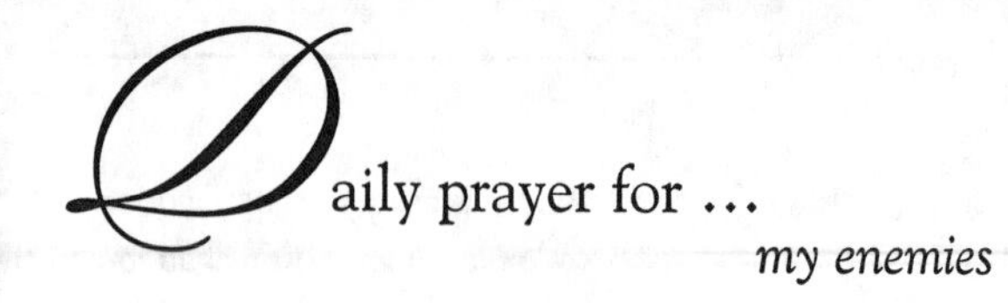

Daily prayer for ...
my enemies

Jesus said, "I'm telling you to love your enemies. Let them bring out the best in you, not the worst."

Matthew 5:44 MSG

Dear Heavenly Father,

There are people in my life who not only are hard to like but seem impossible to love. People who've hurt me, who seem to dislike me for what feels like no reason at all—at least from my point of view.

Help me to better understand their point of view. With Your help, I want to put aside any grudges I'm holding onto and replace those hard feelings with forgiveness. What's impossible for me is possible with You. Please move these relationships in the direction You want them to go. Show me what "loving my enemies" really means.

Amen.

If you see your enemy hungry, go buy him lunch; if he's thirsty, bring him a drink. Your generosity will surprise him with goodness, and GOD will look after you.

Proverbs 25:21, 22 MSG

MY PERSONAL PRAYER

The best way to destroy an enemy is to make him a friend.

Abraham Lincoln

Dear Father:

Amen

Bless your enemies; no cursing under your breath.

Romans 12:14 MSG

When we please the LORD, even our enemies make friends with us.

Proverbs 16:7 CEV

Daily prayer for …

my boss

If you honor your boss, you'll be honored.
Proverbs 27:18 MSG

Dear Heavenly Father,

Please work in my boss's life and in my own. Help me to show the respect due to those You've placed in authority over me. That isn't always easy. Sometimes it seems like my boss makes arbitrary decisions without logic or good sense. At other times, I'm made to feel responsible for poor choices I had no control over.

Show me when to speak and when to remain silent. Let me exhibit Your love and wisdom at my workplace. I want to make a positive difference—both in my work and in the lives of those around me, including my boss. Please help me to be a loving, hard-working example.

Amen.

Work hard and cheerfully at whatever you do, as though you were working for the Lord rather than for people.
Colossians 3:23 NLT

MY PERSONAL PRAYER

There is nothing that makes us love a man so much as praying for him.
William Law

Dear Father:

Amen

Obey your leaders and be under their authority.
Hebrews 13:17 NCV

The mark of a good leader is loyal followers; leadership is nothing without a following.
Proverbs 14:28 MSG

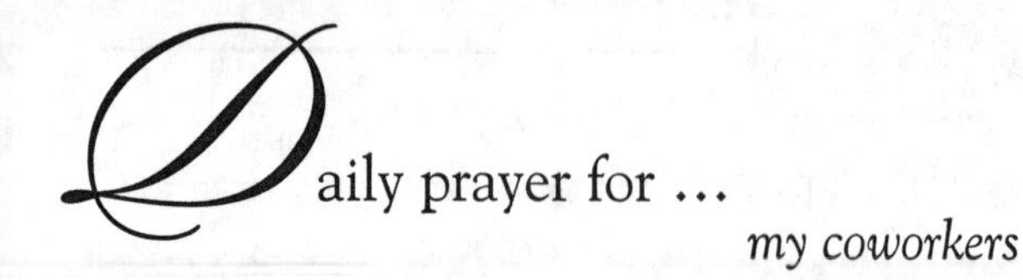

Daily prayer for …
my coworkers

You must love each other as I have loved you.
John 13:34 NCV

Dear Heavenly Father,

Thank You for the people You have placed around me at work. Please make us a team that works well together, a team that doesn't gossip or step on one another to climb higher up the ladder.

As Your child, I want to be an example to my coworkers by doing my job well and showing kindness and cooperation. I can't do that on my own. That's something You need to teach me day by day. Starting today, Lord, bring to mind ways in which I can better love those I work with. Give them a glimpse of Your love through me.

Amen.

Be wise in the way you act with people who are not believers.
Use your time in the best way you can.
Colossians 4:5 NCV

MY PERSONAL PRAYER

Working together is essential for success; even freckles would make a nice tan if they would get together.
Author Unknown

Dear Father:

____

____

____

____

____

____

____

Amen

Don't blow the whistle on your fellow workers behind their backs; They'll accuse you of being underhanded, and then you'll be the guilty one!
Proverbs 30:10 MSG

Settle down and get to work. Earn your own living.
2 Thessalonians 3:12 NLT

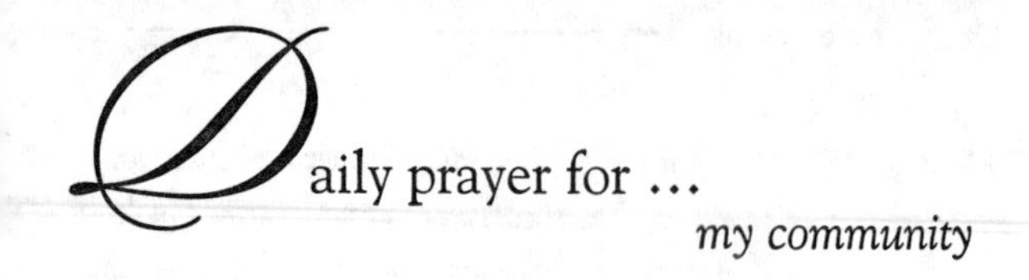

Daily prayer for ...
my community

When right-living people bless the city, it flourishes.

Proverbs 11:11 MSG

Dear Heavenly Father,

I care about the community I live in. I want to be proud of the place I call home. I know I can't just sit back and hope that happens. Prayer is the first step, Lord, and that's why I'm coming to You today.

Work in this city as only You can. Bring godly leaders into positions of power and responsibility, leaders who will run this city with integrity. Then show me what You'd like me to do. How can I put to good use the gifts, abilities, and resources You've given me to make a constructive difference in this community? Help me become Your answer to my own prayer.

Amen.

Don't desecrate the land in which you live. I live here too—I, GOD, live in the same neighborhood.

Numbers 35:34 MSG

MY PERSONAL PRAYER

Only in community can humanity reflect God and fulfill the image of God in which we were created for mutual relationship.

Chung Kyun Kyung

Dear Father:

____

____

____

____

____

____

____

Amen

Unless the Lord protects a city, sentries do no good.

Psalm 127:1 TLB

Clean living before God and justice with our neighbors mean far more to GOD than religious performance.

Proverbs 21:3 MSG

Daily prayer for ...

the poor

Those who oppress the poor insult their Maker,
but those who help the poor honor him.
Proverbs 14:31 NLT

Dear Heavenly Father,

Even when times are tight, I know I'm not poor compared to so many others in this world. Thank You for Your countless blessings in my life. Though I enjoy every one of them, I don't want to hoard them just to make my life easier and more comfortable.

I want my heart to look like Yours—a heart dedicated to sacrifice and service and loving well. Show me how to love well in practical ways. Open my eyes to opportunities—both in my community and around the world—where I can share Your blessings with others who are struggling to make ends meet.

Please use me to take care of the poor, whom You so dearly love.

Amen.

God blesses those who are kind to the poor.
He helps them out of their troubles.
Psalm 41:1 TLB

MY PERSONAL PRAYER

The good Lord has been good to me, and I am just trying to return the favor.

Milton Petrie

Dear Father:

____

____

____

____

____

____

____

Amen

If you stop your ears to the cries of the poor,
your cries will go unheard, unanswered.
Proverbs 21:13 MSG

It's better to live humbly among the poor than to live it up among the rich and famous.
Proverbs 16:19 MSG

Daily prayer for ...

our country

Righteousness exalts a nation.
Proverbs 14:34 NKJV

Dear Heavenly Father,

When I think of our country, I first think of our president and all those who must deal with domestic and international problems in such a volatile world. Be with them in a miraculous way. Give them wisdom. Guide them to make choices that reflect Your heart and concerns. May Your Holy Spirit draw them ever closer to knowing You.

As for me, remind me to not take my nation and my freedoms for granted. Teach me how to be a better and more informed citizen. Help me to vote wisely and do my part in making this country a place I'm proud to call home. May this nation be a shining demonstration of godliness and freedom in this world.

Amen.

When the country is in chaos, everybody has a plan to fix it—
but it takes a leader of real understanding to straighten things out.
Proverbs 28:2 MSG

MY PERSONAL PRAYER

God gives all men all earth to love,
but since man's heart is small,
ordains for each one spot shall
prove beloved over all.
Rudyard Kipling

Dear Father:

Amen

Pray especially for rulers and their governments to rule well
so we can be quietly about our business of living simply.
1 Timothy 2:2 MSG

All kings shall fall down before Him;
all nations shall serve Him.
Psalm 72:11 NKJV

Daily prayer for ...

our world

O Lord our God, the majesty and glory of your name fills all the earth and overflows the heavens.

Psalm 8:1 TLB

Dear Heavenly Father,

The whole world is Yours. So often I get preoccupied with my own little corner and forget the bigger picture. Forgive me. Make me more aware, more concerned, more active in reaching out to the world with Your love and Your message.

Help me to see individuals, not just names of countries on a globe. Awaken the hearts of more of Your children, compelling them to venture to other countries to share Your good news. Show me where I fit into this big picture, how I can use the advantages You've given me by living here to help others who are struggling around the globe.

Amen.

Jesus told his disciples, "Go and make disciples of all the nations, baptizing them in the name of the Father and the Son and the Holy Spirit."

Matthew 28:19 NLT

MY PERSONAL PRAYER

My soul weeps for the whole world.
Staretz Silouan

Dear Father:

Amen

Those who live at the ends of the earth stand in awe of your wonders.
Psalm 65:8 NLT

Praise God, O world! May all the peoples of the earth give thanks to you.
Psalm 67:5 TLB

There is a place where Heaven's resistless power
Responsive moves to thine insistent plea;
There is a place—a silent, trusting hour—
Where God Himself descends and fights for thee.
Where is that blessed place dost thou ask, "Where?"
O soul, it is the secret place of prayer.

Author Unknown

Daily Prayers for Help …

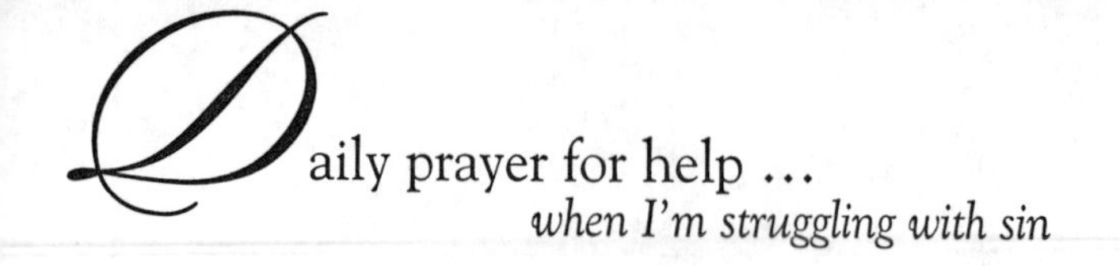

Daily prayer for help …
when I'm struggling with sin

No temptation is irresistible. You can trust God to keep the temptation from becoming so strong that you can't stand up against it.
1 Corinthians 10:13 TLB

Dear Heavenly Father,

I know that I'm Your child. Yet I see so much of myself that does not resemble You—pride, hatred, anger, selfishness, greed, and lust. I know that the more I learn to know You, the more closely I should reflect Your image. But there's still so much of my character that needs Your healing hand—and Your forgiveness.

Strengthen my resolve to choose Your ways over the way others say I should live and act. Reveal to me where sin is clouding my relationship with You. Then help me change. Show me what living a holy life really means—and enable me to live one.

Amen.

You sinners, clean sin out of your lives.
James 4:8 NCV

MY PERSONAL PRAYER

Wounds cannot be healed until they are revealed and sins cannot be forgiven until they are confessed.

Martin Luther

Dear Father:

Amen

O God, you know how foolish I am;
my sins cannot be hidden from you.
Psalm 69:5 NLT

He has removed our sins as far away from us as the east is from the west.
Psalm 103:12 TLB

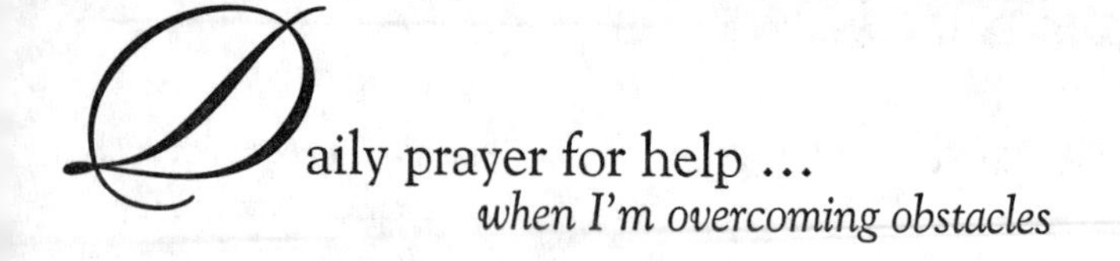

Daily prayer for help ...
when I'm overcoming obstacles

In my distress I cried out to the LORD; yes, I prayed to my God for help. He heard me from his sanctuary; my cry reached his ears.

Psalm 18:6 NLT

Dear Heavenly Father,

This is more than just a problem. This feels almost insurmountable. Of course, I'm just one small person, Lord. But You are one huge God. Help me to see this from Your perspective. Help me to keep my focus on Your power and purpose, Your never-ending love. With You, nothing is impossible.

Please get this obstacle out of my path. Remove it, I pray. If You will not remove it, show me how to go around it, or give me the perseverance I need to chip away at it—to go right through the center of this obstacle. I know You'll be right there with me every step of the way.

Amen.

Do not be afraid or discouraged, for the LORD is the one who goes before you. He will be with you; he will neither fail you nor forsake you.

Deuteronomy 31:8 NLT

MY PERSONAL PRAYER

You cannot think a prayer so large that God, in answering it, will not wish you had made it larger.

Phillips Brooks

Dear Father:

____

____

____

____

____

____

____

Amen

If one of you is having troubles, he should pray.

James 5:13 NCV

Listen closely to my prayer, O LORD; hear my urgent cry. I will call to you whenever trouble strikes, and you will answer me.

Psalm 86:6, 7 NLT

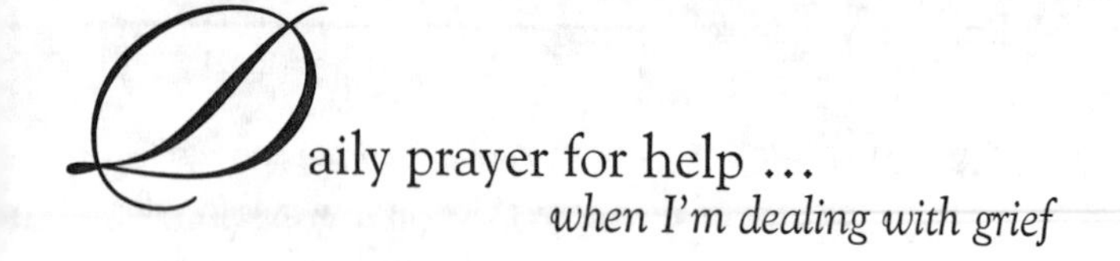

Daily prayer for help ...
when I'm dealing with grief

The LORD is close to the brokenhearted;
he rescues those who are crushed in spirit.
Psalm 34:18 NLT

Dear Heavenly Father,

There's nothing I can do, but cry—and pray. I can hardly think of words to say, the pain cuts so deep. But You know the depth of my grief, the questions and hopelessness that are constricting my heart.

Give me relief, Lord, I pray. Comfort me with Your Word and Your presence. Surround me with trustworthy friends who can be Your hands and feet, friends who can share my tears or just sit with me in silence, if that's what I need at the moment.

Give me the strength to trust in You when it feels as though my world is falling apart. And when my grief has subsided, Lord, add to it Your gifts of hope and peace.

Amen.

I will turn their mourning to joy, will comfort them,
and make them rejoice rather than sorrow.
Jeremiah 31:13 NKJV

MY PERSONAL PRAYER

Earth hath no sorrow that heaven cannot heal.

Thomas Moore

Dear Father:

____

____

____

____

____

____

____

Amen

The LORD's loved ones are precious to him;
it grieves him when they die.
Psalm 116:15 NLT

The Lamb on the Throne will shepherd them, will lead them to spring waters of Life. And God will wipe every last tear from their eyes.
Revelations 7:17 MSG

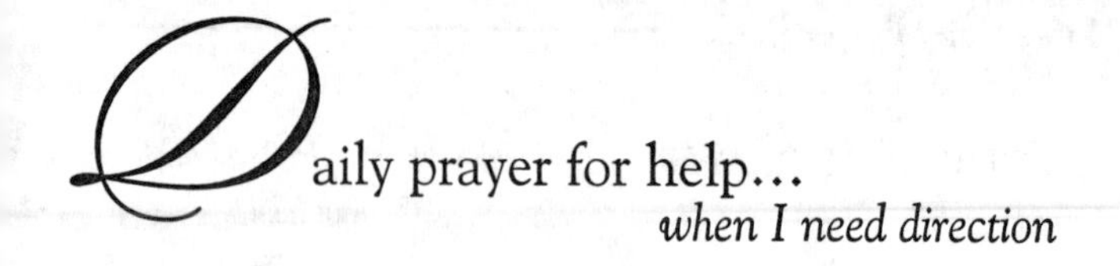

Daily prayer for help...
when I need direction

I'm still in your presence, but you've taken my hand. You wisely and tenderly lead me, and then you bless me.

Psalm 73:23, 24 MSG

Dear Heavenly Father,

I'm not sure which way to go. It feels like I'm at a fork in the road with no map. But I know that Your Holy Spirit and Your Word provide an eternal atlas that will lead me wherever You want me to go. Use them to guide me right now.

Give me peace about what to do and then the courage to move ahead in that direction. Confirm my choice through the advice of those who know You well. You've said You'll provide wisdom to all who ask for it. Lord, and I'm asking. I'm counting on You to fulfill Your precious promise.

Amen.

The LORD will guide you continually, watering your life when you are dry and keeping you healthy, too.

Isaiah 58:11 NLT

MY PERSONAL PRAYER

Faith is the daring of the soul to go farther than it can see.

William Newton Clarke

Dear Father:

____

____

____

____

____

____

____

Amen

I will bless the LORD who guides me;
even at night my heart instructs me.

Psalm 16:7 NLT

In all your ways acknowledge Him,
and He shall direct your paths.

Proverbs 3:6 NKJV

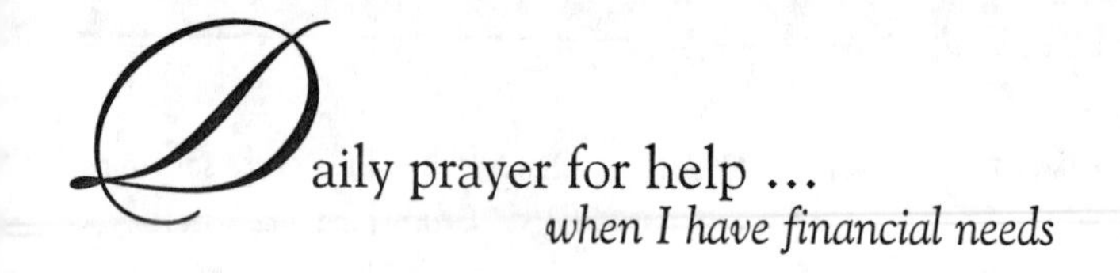

Daily prayer for help ...
when I have financial needs

Jesus said, "Your heavenly Father already knows all your needs, and he will give you all you need from day to day if you live for him and make the Kingdom of God your primary concern."
Matthew 6:32, 33 NLT

Dear Heavenly Father,

Money seems like such an unspiritual thing to ask of You. And yet I know that You care about every detail of my life—including my finances. Please provide me with what I need in whatever way You determine is best.

Help me to better understand what I can do personally to change the direction of this situation. Show me how to continue being generous with others when I feel as though I don't have enough for myself. Teach me to better discern my needs from my wants and live within the means You provide—whatever those means may be. Lead me toward joy and contentment, regardless of what tax bracket I'm in.

Amen.

My God will use his wonderful riches in Christ Jesus to give you everything you need.
Philippians 4:19 NCV

MY PERSONAL PRAYER

Pray as though everything depended on God. Work as though everything depended on you.

Saint Augustine

Dear Father:

____

____

____

____

____

____

____

Amen

Keep your lives free from the love of money, and be satisfied with what you have. God has said, "I will never leave you; I will never forget you."

Hebrews 13:5 NCV

The Lord's blessing is our greatest wealth. All our work adds nothing to it!

Proverbs 10:22 TLB

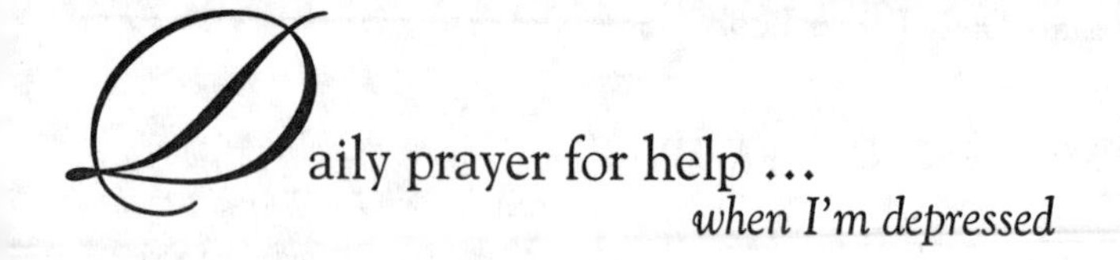

Daily prayer for help …
when I'm depressed

"Who will give me wings," I ask—"wings like a dove?" Get me out of here on dove wings; I want some peace and quiet.

Psalm 55:67 MSG

Dear Heavenly Father,

My heart feels so heavy. I feel as though there's nothing I can do to bring joy back into my life. It's more than just circumstances. It goes deeper than that, Lord. Something is wrong inside that I can't fix. But I know that You can see the root of the problem. You can see it, and You can heal it with Your comforting touch.

Do that now, Lord. I need You. If I need to see a doctor or counselor, confirm that in my heart. If I need to make other changes, show me that as well. Just help me find my way back to a place of balance, where Your joy is close at hand. Bring light into my darkness, I pray.

Amen.

As pressure and stress bear down on me, I find joy in your commands.

Psalm 119:143 NLT

MY PERSONAL PRAYER

The refiner is never very far from the mouth of the furnace when his gold is in the fire.

Charles Haddon Spurgeon

Dear Father:

____

____

____

____

____

____

____

Amen

When my soul is in the dumps, I rehearse everything I know about you.

Psalm 42:6 MSG

I know the LORD is always with me. I will not be shaken, for he is right beside me.

Psalm 16:8 NLT

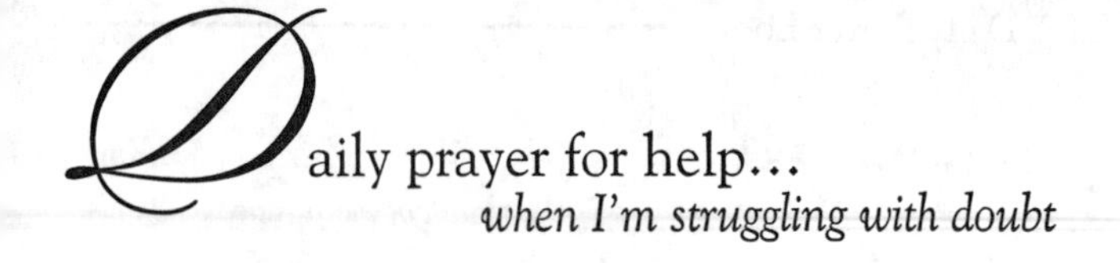

Daily prayer for help...
when I'm struggling with doubt

The word of the LORD holds true, and everything he does is worthy of our trust.
Psalm 33:4 NLT

Dear Heavenly Father,

I know that You won't answer every question I have in this life. But some of my questions feel like stumbling blocks that are keeping me from drawing closer to You. I need You to help me remove them.

Dissolve any doubts that are simply the worries and struggles of an unfocused mind. Help me find answers to the questions that I'm not able to understand in this life. Then give me the courage to move forward in faith, even when all my doubts have not disappeared. I want to trust You, no matter what. Please show me how.

Amen.

Trust in the LORD with all your heart,
and lean not on your own understanding.
Proverbs 3:5 NKJV

MY PERSONAL PRAYER

Never doubt in the dark what God told you in the light.
V. Raymond Edman

Dear Father:

Amen

Go easy on those who hesitate in the faith.
Jude 22 MSG

Lord, when doubts fill my mind, when my heart is in turmoil, quiet me and give me renewed hope and cheer.
Psalm 94:19 TLB

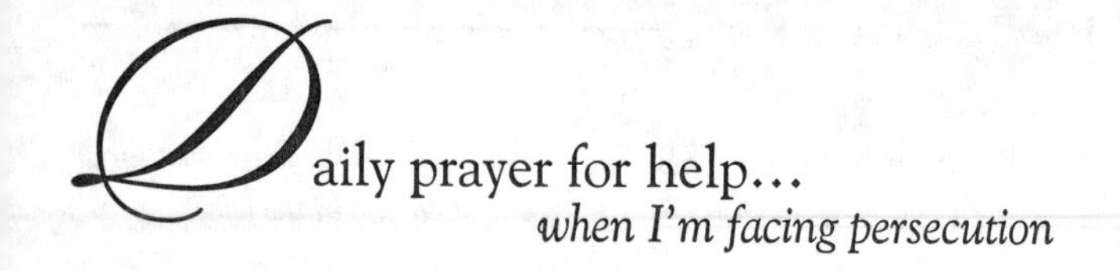

Daily prayer for help...
when I'm facing persecution

If someone mistreats you because you are a Christian, don't curse him; pray that God will bless him.

Romans 12:14 TLB

Dear Heavenly Father,

I know there's a spiritual struggle going on in this world, a battle to keep people from believing in You. As one of Your children, I'm caught in the crossfire. When people persecute me, it's because they're fighting their own battle to connect with You.

Give me the strength to keep reaching out to others and sharing what I know about You—even if my words open me up to ridicule or rejection. Make me more sensitive to Your Spirit's guidance when I speak and when I listen. Remind me to wrap every conversation in prayer. It's You, not my simple words, that have the power to change a person's destiny.

Amen.

Jesus said, "Since they persecuted me, naturally they will persecute you."

John 15:20 NLT

MY PERSONAL PRAYER

Christ's followers cannot expect better treatment in the world than their Master had.

Matthew Henry

Dear Father:

Amen

Jesus said, "God blesses those who are persecuted because they live for God, for the Kingdom of Heaven is theirs."

Matthew 5:10 NLT

Being reviled, we bless; being persecuted, we endure.

1 Corinthians 4:12 NKJV

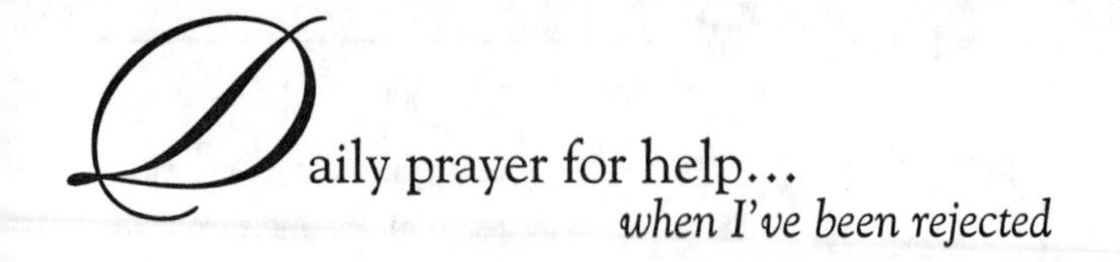

Daily prayer for help…
when I've been rejected

Overlook an offense and bond a friendship;
fasten on to a slight and—goodbye, friend!
Proverbs 17:9 MSG

Dear Heavenly Father,

Jesus was rejected by those who once followed Him. He was betrayed by the kiss of a friend. He was abandoned by those He loved, even though He'd done nothing wrong. Your Son knows what it's like to be wounded by those He trusted. And so do I.

Grief, disbelief, and anger are all swirling around inside me, and I'm not quite sure what to do. I need Your help in sorting everything out. Only You can prevent bitterness from taking root in my heart.

Part of me wants to strike back. The other part wants to respond as Jesus did, with love and forgiveness. I pray that You'll give me the strength to follow in Jesus' footsteps, to do the right thing.

Amen.

Even if my father and mother abandon me,
the LORD will hold me close.
Psalm 27:10 NLT

MY PERSONAL PRAYER

God sometimes snuffs out our brightest candle so that we may look up to His eternal stars.

Vance Havner

Dear Father:

Amen

Jesus Christ is the living stone that people have rejected, but which God has chosen and highly honored.

1 Peter 2:4 CEV

Jesus is despised and rejected by men, a Man of sorrows and acquainted with grief.

Isaiah 53:3 NKJV

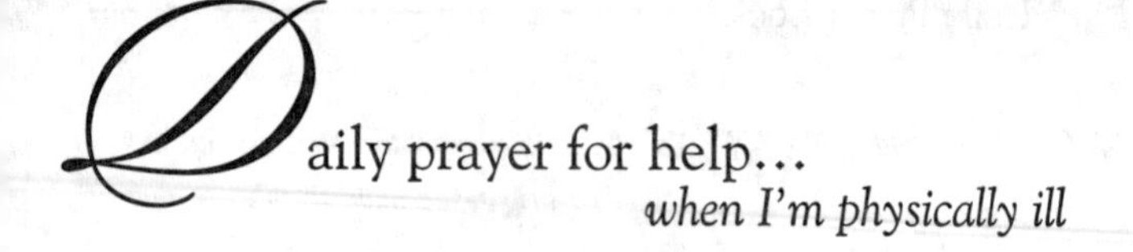

Daily prayer for help...
when I'm physically ill

My health may fail, and my spirit may grow weak, but God remains the strength of my heart; he is mine forever.

Psalm 73:26 NLT

Dear Heavenly Father,

You are the Great Physician, the Almighty Healer, my Comforter, and my Friend. Please make Your presence known to me in a special way right now. Touch my body with Your healing power. Revive my energy and ease my pain.

And, Lord, if it's Your plan that my body not be healed at this time, then give me the patience and perseverance I need to watch and wait. Show me how to use my time well when I don't feel up to accomplishing what's usually on my "To Do" list. Teach me how to be still and find comfort in simply knowing that You are God—and that I am loved.

Amen.

Are any among you sick? They should call for the elders of the church and have them pray over them.

James 5:14 NLT

MY PERSONAL PRAYER

In time of sickness,
the soul collects itself anew.
Latin Proverb

Dear Father:

Amen

I am the LORD who heals you.
Exodus 15:26 NKJV

God is my helper. The Lord is the one who keeps me alive!
Psalm 54:4 NLT

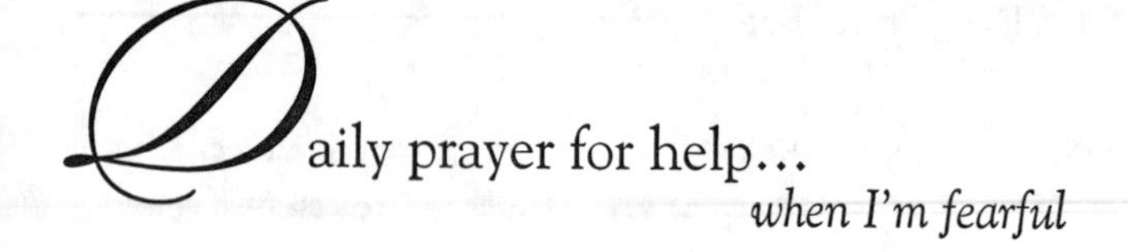

Daily prayer for help... *when I'm fearful*

Don't be afraid, for I am with you. Do not be dismayed, for I am your God.

Isaiah 41:10 NLT

Dear Heavenly Father,

In Your Word, You said that "perfect love casts out fear." I need Your perfect love to calm my fears right now. I know that nothing happens in my life that is out of Your sight or control. At least my mind knows that's true. But somehow my heart is still hanging onto fear.

Please release me from that fear, Lord. Let Your truth calm my heart as I consider how big You are and how small the object of my fear really is. Give me the courage to move forward and face what I'm afraid of, knowing that You're right there beside me, holding my hand, ready to defend me.

Amen.

Jesus said, "Don't be afraid. Just believe."

Mark 5:36 NIV

MY PERSONAL PRAYER

Courage is fear that has said its prayers.
Dorothy Bernard

Dear Father:

Amen

The LORD is my light and my salvation; whom shall I fear?
Psalm 27:1 NKJV

I prayed to the LORD and he answered me,
freeing me from all my fears.
Psalm 34:4 NLT

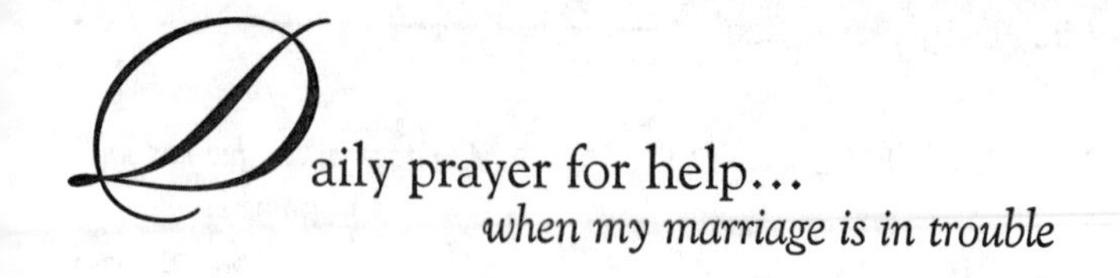

Daily prayer for help…
when my marriage is in trouble

Marriage is not a place to "stand up for your rights." Marriage is a decision to serve the other.
1 Corinthians 7:4 MSG

Dear Heavenly Father,

The relationship that I thought would bring me the most joy in life is now the source of my greatest heartache. I don't want to stay here, God. I don't want to settle for just putting up with the way things are. I want the two of us to honor You with our lives and with our love, together as a couple.

Soften my heart so that I can consciously make the most of opportunities for sacrifice and forgiveness, regardless of how my spouse responds. Teach me how to love the way You do—completely, unselfishly. And give me the courage to release my marriage, my spouse, and myself into Your capable hands.

Amen.

What you say can preserve life or destroy it; so you must accept the consequences of your words.
Proverbs 18:21 GNT

MY PERSONAL PRAYER

A successful marriage requires falling in love many times, always with the same person.

Mignon McLaughlin

Dear Father:

____

____

____

____

____

____

____

Amen

As iron sharpens iron, so one person sharpens another.

Proverbs 27:17 NIrV

Bear one another's burdens.

Galatians 6:2 NKJV

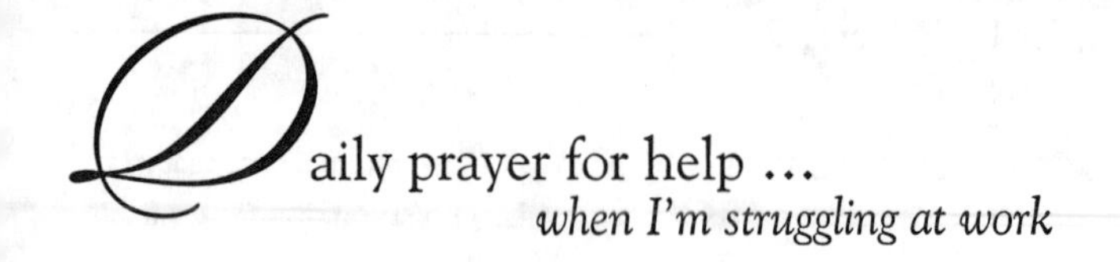

Daily prayer for help ...
when I'm struggling at work

To enjoy your work and accept your lot in life—that is indeed a gift from God.
Ecclesiastes 5:19 NLT

Dear Heavenly Father,

Right now I'm so frustrated with my job. Yes, Lord, the same one I was once so excited about getting. Help me to step back a little bit, take a deep breath, and remember how it was at the beginning. I also want to stop and thank You for my job—I know full well that it's a blessing no matter how difficult it might seem at times. It is Your provision for our family and supplies us with the income we need.

Lord, I recommit my job to You. Give me the strength to work with excellence, even when I don't feel like it. Help me to speak honestly and always give my best.

Amen.

GOD cares about honesty in the workplace; your business is his business.
Proverbs 16:11 MSG

MY PERSONAL PRAYER

He who labors as he prays lifts up his heart to God with his hands.
Saint Bernard of Clairvaux

Dear Father:

Amen

All goes well for the generous man who conducts his business fairly.
Psalm 112:5 TLB

Stay calm; mind your own business; do your own job.
1 Thessalonians 4:11 MSG

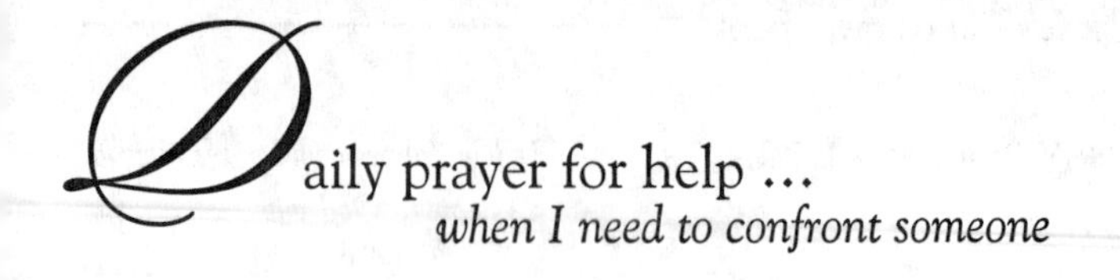

Daily prayer for help …
when I need to confront someone

We will lovingly follow the truth at all times—speaking truly, dealing truly, living truly.

Ephesians 4:15 TLB

Dear Heavenly Father,

I know what needs to be said, yet I wish I wasn't the one who had to say it. But I treasure truth and right relationships more than my own comfort. So I'm ready to speak the words that I feel You want me to say.

Help me to speak words that are wise and gentle. Let Your truth be the sword that cuts through the problem. Please calm my personal emotions, as well as the emotions of the one I'm speaking to, so that what I'm saying won't be perceived as a critical judgment. Instead, may every word come across as a gift of love from someone who cares enough to confront.

Amen.

Love each other as if your life depended on it. Love makes up for practically anything.

1 Peter 4:8 MSG

MY PERSONAL PRAYER

Friends, if we be honest with ourselves, we shall be honest with each other.

George MacDonald

Dear Father:

Amen

An honest answer is like a warm hug.

Proverbs 24:26 MSG

Honest people are relaxed and confident, bold as lions.

Proverbs 28:1 MSG

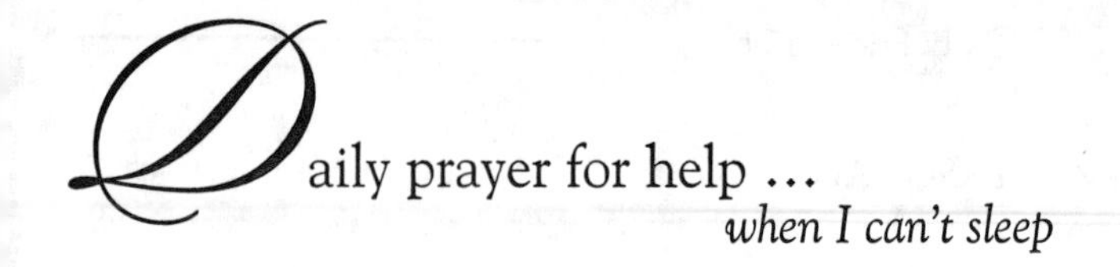

Daily prayer for help ...
when I can't sleep

It is useless to work so hard for a living, getting up early and going to bed late. For the LORD provides for those he loves, while they are asleep.

Psalm 127:2 GNT

Dear Heavenly Father,

I'm exhausted—but I can't sleep. Please calm my mind and my body. Bring me Your peace in a physical, tangible way. Relax my muscles, from head to toe. Ease any tension and worry that is in my mind.

If there's a problem or prayer I need to bring to You, please reveal it to me right now. Help me to place it in Your hands and then roll over and find real rest in Your arms.

It isn't for me to know what tomorrow holds—it will come soon enough and we will face it together. Please give me the energy I need to tackle tomorrow, starting with the gift of a good night's sleep.

Amen.

If I'm sleepless at midnight, I spend the hours in grateful reflection.

Psalm 63:6 MSG

MY PERSONAL PRAYER

Prayer should be the key of the day and the lock of the night.
Thomas Fuller

Dear Father:

____

____

____

____

____

____

____

Amen

God will never let me stumble, slip or fall. For he is always watching, never sleeping.
Psalm 121:3, 4 TLB

At day's end I'm ready for sound sleep, for you, GOD, have put my life back together.
Psalm 4:8 MSG

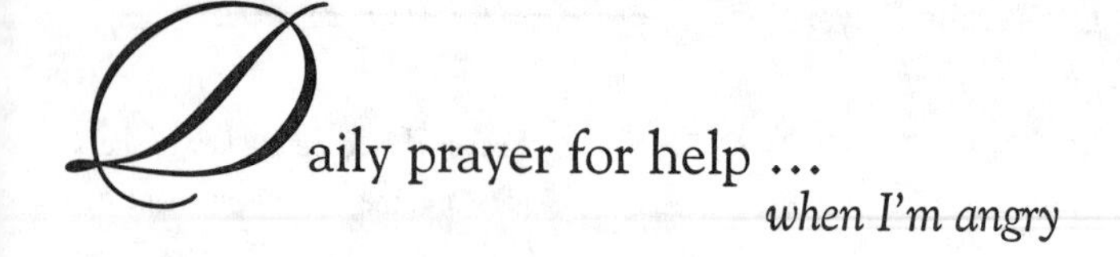

Daily prayer for help … *when I'm angry*

Be careful that when you get on each other nerves you don't snap at each other. Look for the best in each other, and always do your best to bring it out.

1 Thessalonians 5:15 MSG

Dear Heavenly Father,

I am so angry that I feel I have to do something! Instead of arguing, complaining, gossiping, or wallowing in bitterness, I've chosen to talk to You. Please honor that choice, Lord.

Release this anger from my heart. Show me the truth behind this situation, including where I may have been wrong. Then help me do what I need to do to make things right. Help me know how to resolve this problem in a practical way that reconciles relationships and brings glory to You. At this point, I'm not sure how all of that should take place, but I want to be a peacemaker. Calm my emotions and clear my mind so Your wisdom can guide me.

Amen.

Do not become angry easily. Anger will not help you live a good life as God wants.

James 1:19, 20 NCV

MY PERSONAL PRAYER

Anger is a wind which blows out the lamp of the mind.
Robert G. Ingersoll

Dear Father:

Amen

Love does not demand its own way. Love is not irritable, and it keeps no record of when it has been wronged.
1 Corinthians 13:5 NLT

I am the LORD, the merciful and gracious God. I am slow to anger and rich in unfailing love and faithfulness.
Exodus 34:6 NLT

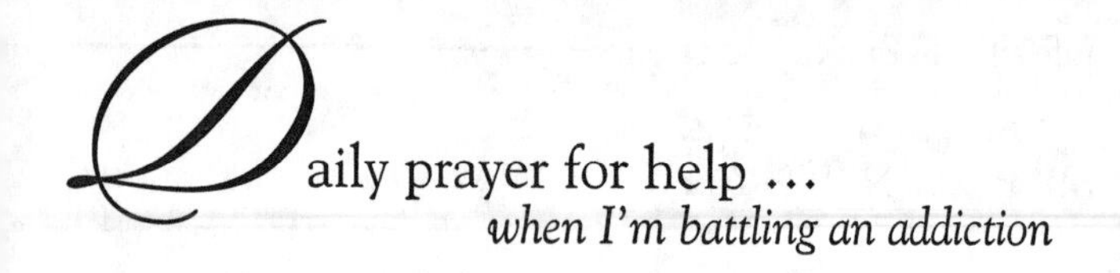

Daily prayer for help … *when I'm battling an addiction*

Get down on your knees before the Master;
it's the only way you'll get on your feet.
James 4:10 MSG

Dear Heavenly Father,

I'm fighting a battle that I know I can't win on my own. Please fight for me. Strengthen my self-control and resolve. Protect me from situations that would tempt me to go back to my old habits. Teach me how to better rely on You, instead of relying on this false god I've become dependent on. Show me the path to freedom.

I know it won't be easy. I know that You and I will probably have to fight this same battle again tomorrow. But I'm willing to commit myself, day by day, to breaking the hold of this addiction in my life if You will help me, Lord.

Amen.

Be prepared. You're up against far more
than you can handle on your own.
Ephesians 6:13 MSG

MY PERSONAL PRAYER

What makes resisting temptation difficult, for many people, is that they don't want to discourage it completely.

Franklin P. Jones

Dear Father:

Amen

God's Word is an indispensable weapon.

Ephesians 6:17 MSG

We use God's mighty weapons, not mere worldly weapons, to knock down the Devil's strongholds.

2 Corinthians 10:4 NLT

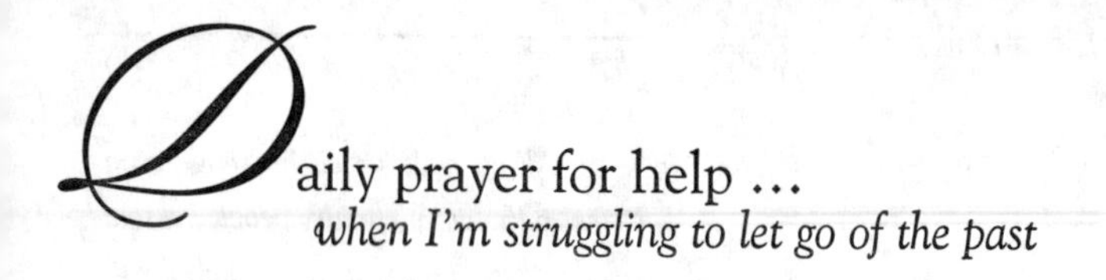

Daily prayer for help ...
when I'm struggling to let go of the past

Forget the things that happened in the past.
Do not keep thinking about them.
Isaiah 43:18 NIrV

Dear Heavenly Father,

I know that You won't change the past, but You can change how I look at it. That's what I'm asking for now. Heal my past hurts. Help me to let go of any bitterness, while tightly clinging to Your promise that You'll bring good out of every circumstance according to Your purpose. Encourage my heart with a glimpse of the good You have planned.

I don't want yesterday to steal any more joy from today—or tomorrow. Show me what I need to do, how I need to pray, and who I need to talk to, so I can move forward with my head held high and heart set free.

Amen.

God is greater than our worried hearts and knows
more about us than we do ourselves.
1 John 3:20 MSG

MY PERSONAL PRAYER

In Christ we can move out of our past into a meaningful present and a breathtaking future.
Erwin W. Lutzer

Dear Father:

Amen

My eyes strain to see your deliverance,
to see the truth of your promise fulfilled.
Psalm 119:123 NLT

God says, "I am about to do a new thing;
now it springs forth, do you not perceive it?"
Isaiah 43:19 NRSV

Before us is a future all unknown,
a path untrod;
Beside us a friend well loved and known—
That friend is God.

Author Unknown

Daily Prayers for Guidance …

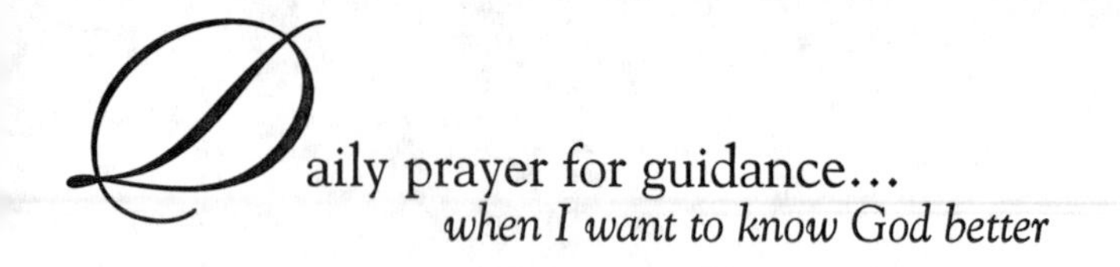

Daily prayer for guidance...
when I want to know God better

Jesus said, "This is the way to eternal life—to know you, the only true God, and Jesus Christ, the one you sent to earth."
John 17:3 NLT

Dear Heavenly Father,

I don't want to just know about You. I want to really know You—personally, intimately, and experientially. But I'm not quite sure how to do that with someone I can't really see or hear. Please teach me.

Through Your words in the Bible, the power of Your Spirit, and my deep-hearted prayers, draw us closer together as Father and child. Help me to better understand Your heart and what being a holy God really means, through obedience, worship, and just spending time in Your presence. Day by day, draw me more deeply into relationship with You. Hold me ever-more tightly in Your arms.

Amen.

"When you call on me, when you come and pray to me, I'll listen. When you come looking for me, you'll find me."
Jeremiah 29:12, 13 MSG

MY PERSONAL PRAYER

Love clings to Christ even when the intellect cannot understand.
William Barclay

Dear Father:

Amen

Be still, and know that I am God.
Psalm 46:10 NKJV

Everything else is worthless when compared with the priceless gain of knowing Christ Jesus my Lord.
Philippians 3:8 NLT

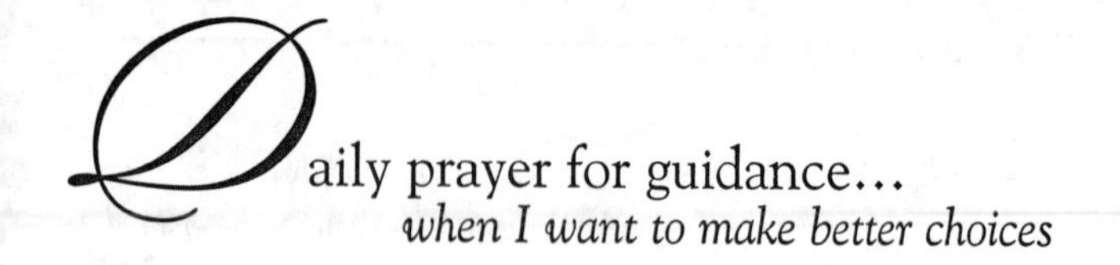

Daily prayer for guidance…
when I want to make better choices

Knowing what is right is like deep water in the heart; a wise person draws from the well within.

Proverbs 20:5 MSG

Dear Heavenly Father,

There are so many seemingly insignificant choices I make every day, such as how I spend a few dollars, what I decide to feed my body, the tone of voice with which I choose to speak to those I love. Yet I know that even the smallest of these decisions can be influenced for better or worse by how closely I happen to be following You.

I want every choice I make to be one that You can be proud of. I need Your wisdom to discern what that means in every area of my life. Slow me down so I can be more deliberate about the decisions I make… and so I can hear Your voice more clearly.

Amen.

Choose my instruction rather than silver, and knowledge over pure gold.

Proverbs 8:10 NLT

MY PERSONAL PRAYER

Every day the choice between good and evil is presented to us in simple ways.
William Edwyn Robert Sangster

Dear Father:

____

____

____

____

____

____

____

Amen

Stand ready to help me, for I have chosen to follow your commandments.
Psalm 119:173 NLT

Jesus said, "If any of you wants to be my follower, you must put aside your selfish ambition, shoulder my cross, and follow me."
Matthew 16:24 NLT

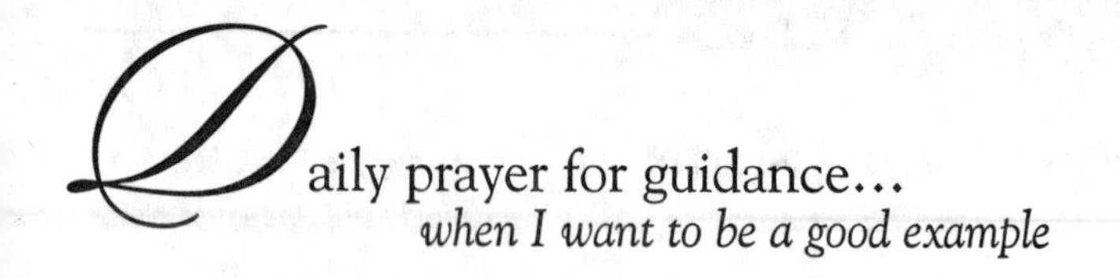

Daily prayer for guidance...
when I want to be a good example

Be an example to all believers in what you teach, in the way you live, in your love, your faith, and your purity.

1 Timothy 4:12 NLT

Dear Heavenly Father,

Every day, what I do preaches a sermon to those around me. Please help me to make that message one that honors You. Let me practice with my actions what I preach with my words and believe in my heart.

I want to pursue excellence in every area of my life—even though I know that pursuing excellence does not always mean I'll achieve it. Help me to be a good example even when I fail. Give me the courage to be open about my faults and failings in a way that clearly points to my dependence on You. Keep me humble and hopeful, an example of an obedient child who is unconditionally loved.

Amen.

Your very lives are a letter that anyone can read by just looking at you. Christ himself wrote it—not with ink, but with God's living Spirit.

2 Corinthians 3:2, 3 MSG

MY PERSONAL PRAYER

The first great gift we can bestow on others is a good example.
Thomas Morell

Dear Father:

Amen

Worship the Lord with the beauty of holy lives.
Psalm 96:9 TLB

Live well, live wisely, live humbly. It's the way you live, not the way you talk, that counts.
James 3:13 MSG

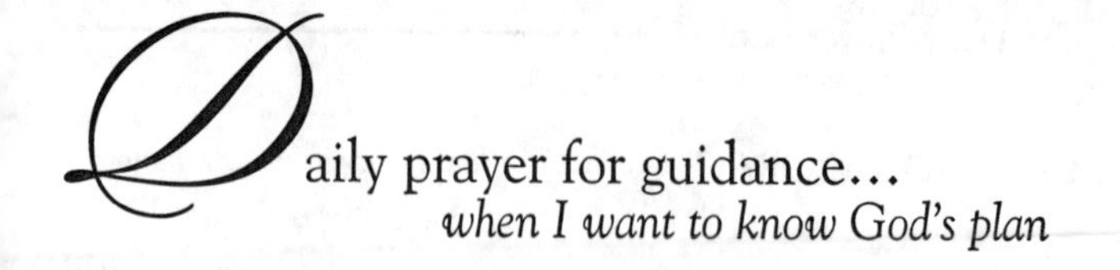

Daily prayer for guidance…

when I want to know God's plan

I know the plans I have for you, says the Lord. They are plans for good and not for evil, to give you a future and a hope.

Jeremiah 29:11 TLB

Dear Heavenly Father,

I know that Your plan for my life unfolds day by day, but I need Your big picture right now. I need to know which way I should go in order to best fulfill the purpose You've laid out for me.

At the heart of that purpose, who I am is ultimately more important than what I do. So please continue to make me more like You, tempering my pride with humility and my humanity with holiness. I want my life to have an impact on the world around me—an impact that has Your fingerprints of love all over it.

Amen.

Where you are right now is God's place for you. Live and obey and love and believe right there.

1 Corinthians 7:17 MSG

MY PERSONAL PRAYER

The strength of a man consists in finding out the way in which God is going, and going that way too.

Henry Ward Beecher

Dear Father:

____

____

____

____

____

____

____

Amen

The One I've trusted in can take care of what he's trusted me to do right to the end.

2 Timothy 1:12 MSG

You will keep on guiding me all my life with your wisdom and counsel.

Psalm 73:24 TLB

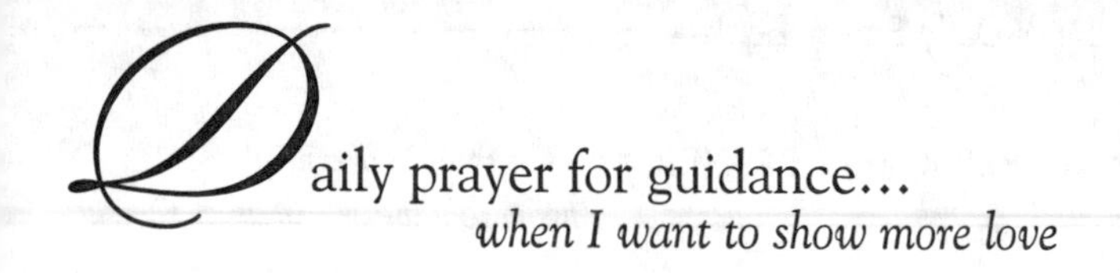

Daily prayer for guidance…
when I want to show more love

Jesus answered, " 'Love the Lord your God with all your heart, soul, and mind.' This is the first and greatest commandment. A second is equally important: 'Love your neighbor as yourself.' "

Matthew 22:37 NLT

Dear Heavenly Father,

Your love is so different from my own. Mine seems to fluctuate with my emotions, with my circumstances, and with how I'm treated by others. Yours remains unchangeable, unfailing, and unconditional. I want to love like You.

Deepen my love for my family, friends, and neighbors. Help my love for You to influence the way I treat the person who serves me a cup of coffee—or cuts me off on the freeway. Extend my love to reach beyond this country's borders to people around the world. Show me how to love extravagantly, and sacrificially, every day of my life.

Amen.

You can develop a healthy, robust community that lives right with God and enjoy its results only if you do the hard work of getting along with each other.

James 3:18 MSG

MY PERSONAL PRAYER

Someday, after mastering the winds, the waves, the tides and gravity, we shall harness for God the energies of love, and then, for the second time in the history of the world, man will discover fire.

Pierre Teilhard de Chardin

Dear Father:

Amen

Work at getting along with each other and with God.

Hebrews 12:14 MSG

Love never gives up, never loses faith, is always hopeful, and endures through every circumstance. Love will last forever.

1 Corinthians 13:7, 8 NLT

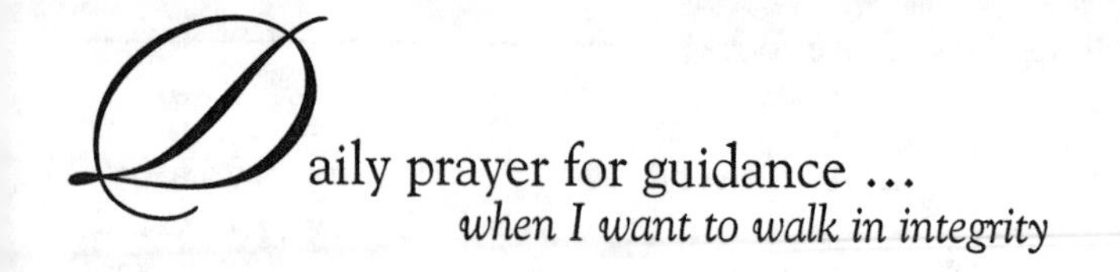

Daily prayer for guidance ...
when I want to walk in integrity

People with integrity have firm footing,
but those who follow crooked paths will slip and fall.

Proverbs 10:9 NLT

Dear Heavenly Father,

I know that integrity isn't considered something of real value these days. It's as though choosing to lead a moral life by obeying You automatically makes me weak and naïve in the world's eyes. But I know that just the opposite is true.

Please give me the strength to go against the grain, to make right choices even when they may not be the most popular. Help my character to better reflect Yours by helping me face any area in my life where honesty, purity, humility, and love are not evident. Cleanse my heart, so I can walk with integrity regardless of whether anyone is watching.

Amen.

Don't copy the behavior and customs of this world, but let God transform you into a new person by changing the way you think.

Romans 12:2 NLT

MY PERSONAL PRAYER

There is no such thing as a minor lapse of integrity.

Tom Peters

Dear Father:

Amen

My dear friends, don't let public opinion influence how you live out our glorious, Christ-originated faith.

James 2:1 MSG

Let integrity and uprightness preserve me, for I wait for You.

Psalm 25:21 NKJV

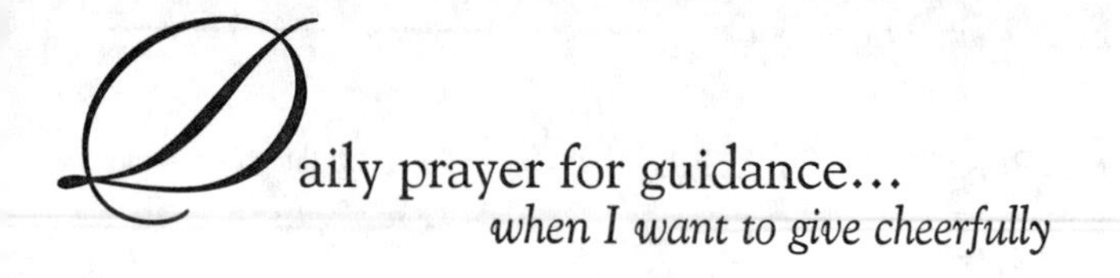

Daily prayer for guidance…
when I want to give cheerfully

Don't give reluctantly or in response to pressure. For God loves the person who gives cheerfully.

2 Corinthians 9:7 NLT

Dear Heavenly Father,

I want to give with the same measure of generosity that You've shown me. But You know that doesn't come naturally. Free my heart from holding too tightly to my money, my possessions, and my time.

Teach me how to reach out to others—especially those in need—in tangible ways. Stretch my comfort zone so I can give cheerfully, as well as sacrificially. I want to give at the right place and the right time with the right motives. I need Your wisdom to do that.

Prevent me from giving out of a need for recognition or a desire to be blessed by others. Let love be at the heart of every gift I give.

Amen.

Tell those rich in this world's wealth to quit being so full of themselves… to do good, to be rich in helping others, to be extravagantly generous.

1 Timothy 6:17, 18 MSG

MY PERSONAL PRAYER

We make a living by what we get.
We make a life by what we give.
Winston Churchill

Dear Father:

Amen

The world of the generous gets larger and larger; the world of the stingy gets smaller and smaller.
Proverbs 11:24 MSG

Give your gifts in secret, and your Father, who knows all secrets, will reward you.
Matthew 6:4 NLT

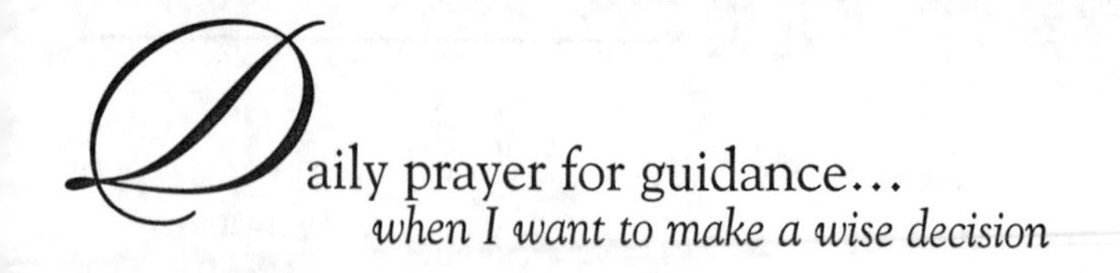

Daily prayer for guidance…
when I want to make a wise decision

Grow a wise heart—you'll do yourself a favor; keep a clear head—you'll find a good life.

Proverbs 19:8 MSG

Dear Heavenly Father,

I want to do more than just make a good decision. I want to make a wise decision—a decision that will lead me in the direction You would most want me to go. Please take all of the knowledge I've accumulated over the years about You, about myself, and about life in general and temper it with the kind of wisdom that I know comes straight from heaven. Help me to weigh the advice of friends according to how it coincides with Your Word.

Then lead me forward with confidence. I want to lean on Your wisdom, and not my own limited understanding, every step of the way.

Amen.

Lucky the men and women who work for you, getting to be around you every day and hear your wise words firsthand!

1 Kings 10:8 MSG

MY PERSONAL PRAYER

O Lord, may I be directed what to do and what to leave undone.

Elizabeth Fry

Dear Father:

____

____

____

____

____

____

____

Amen

We never really know enough until we recognize that God alone knows it all.

1 Corinthians 8:3 MSG

Choose for yourselves whom you will serve. But as for me and my house, we will serve the LORD.

Joshua 24:15 NKJV

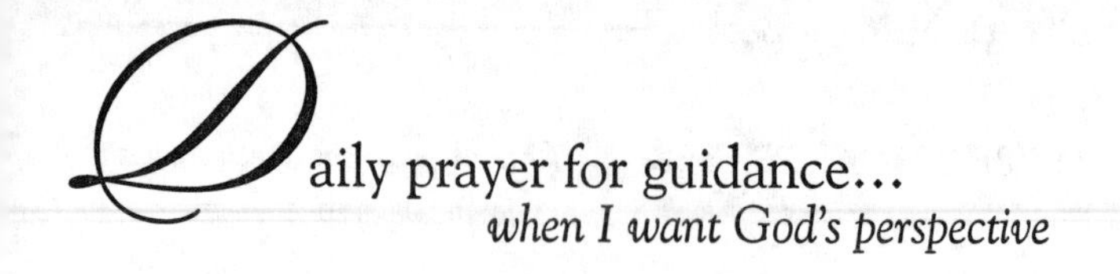

Daily prayer for guidance...
when I want God's perspective

Keep your eyes open for GOD, watch for his works; be alert for signs of his presence.
Psalm 105:4 MSG

Dear Heavenly Father,

My eyesight is far from 20/20 when it comes to seeing things from Your point of view. But I long for Your perspective in every aspect of my life. Help me to view my purpose, other people, and every situation—both good and bad—through Your wise and loving eyes.

Too often my emotions, the opinions of others, and my desire to be happy end up being my guide. The only Guide I want or need is Your Spirit and Your Word. Show me how to look at every situation and decision in light of eternity, rather than what feels right at the moment. Teach me how to think more like You.

Amen.

It's important to look at things from God's point of view.
1 Corinthians 4:6 MSG

MY PERSONAL PRAYER

Every time we pray our horizon is altered, our attitude to things is altered, not sometimes but every time, and the amazing thing is that we don't pray more.

Oswald Chambers

Dear Father:

Amen

Look up, and be alert to what is going on around Christ—that's where the action is. See things from his perspective.

Colossians 3:2 MSG

It's in Christ that we find out who we are and what we are living for.

Ephesians 1:11 MSG

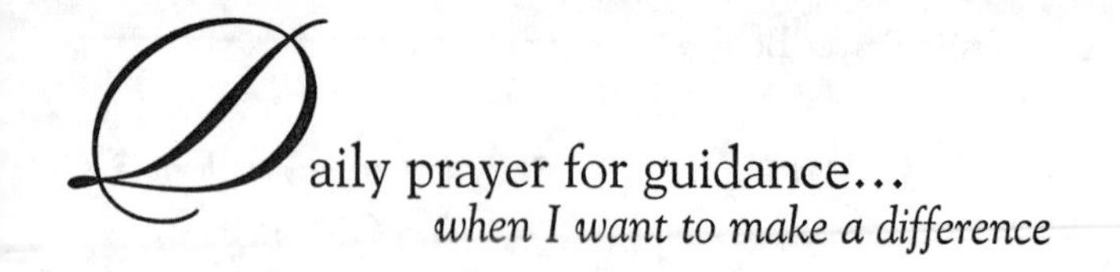

Daily prayer for guidance…
when I want to make a difference

The person who lives in right relationship with God does it by embracing what God arranges for him.

Galatians 3:11 MSG

Dear Heavenly Father,

I want my life to count. I want to invest my time, my energy, and my heart into things that really matter, into what is of eternal value. But I need Your help in figuring out exactly what those things are.

Please help me get to know myself on an even deeper level, to better understand my strengths and my weaknesses. Show me how my life fits into the big picture of eternity.

I want Your purpose to be my purpose. Encourage my heart, so I will be more willing to take risks and choose rocky paths, when I know they are choices You want me to make—choices that will make a difference for You in this world.

Amen.

Pray that God will fill your good ideas and acts of faith with his own energy so that it all amounts to something.

2 Thessalonians 1:11 MSG

MY PERSONAL PRAYER

Attempt great things for God.
Expect great things from God.
William Carey

Dear Father:

____

____

____

____

____

____

____

Amen

Never be lazy in your work,
but serve the Lord enthusiastically.
Romans 12:11 NLT

What you say about yourself means nothing in God's work.
It's what God says about you that makes the difference.
2 Corinthians 10:18 MSG

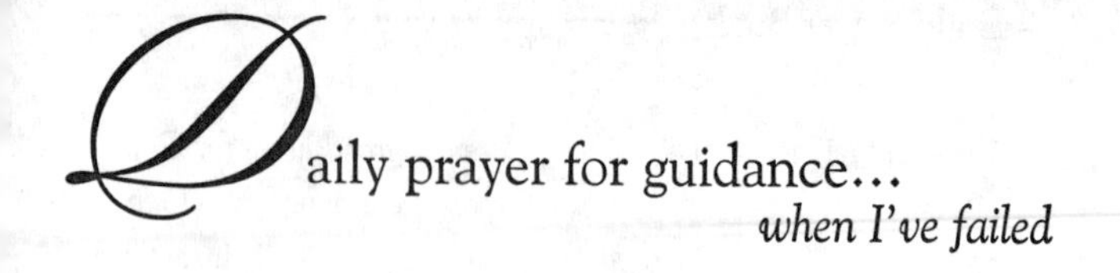

Daily prayer for guidance...
when I've failed

Refuse good advice and watch your plans fail;
take good counsel and watch them succeed.
Proverbs 15:22 MSG

Dear Heavenly Father,

You never fail me. Even when You don't answer my prayers in the way I want You to, I know that I can trust Your love and Your promises to do the right thing in light of eternity. I need that perspective now.

Unlike You, I fail all too often. I know that's part of being human. But it hurts my pride and throws my personal plans into chaos. Letting You, myself, and others down is never part of my plan—but maybe it is part of Yours. Let me learn from this time, Lord. Give me the courage to reevaluate where I'm going, and then try again. Let my success rely on Your perfect timing and Your plan.

Amen.

Humble yourselves under the mighty power of God,
and in his good time he will honor you.
1 Peter 5:6 NLT

MY PERSONAL PRAYER

God is a specialist: he is well able to work our failures into his plans... Often the doorway to success is entered through the hallway of failure.

Erwin W. Lutzer

Dear Father:

____

____

____

____

____

____

____

Amen

My flesh and my heart fail; but God is the strength of my heart and my portion forever.

Psalm 73:26 NKJV

Let your unfailing love comfort me, just as you promised me.

Psalm 119:76 NLT

When all thy mercies, O my God!
My rising soul surveys,
Transported with the view, I'm lost
In wonder, love, and praise.

Joseph Addison

Daily Prayers of Praise …

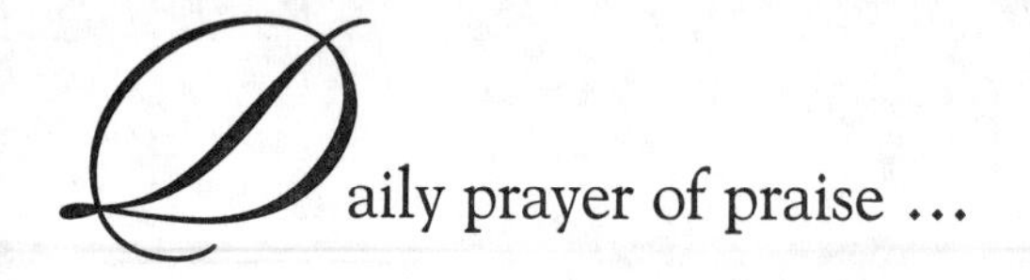

Daily prayer of praise ... *for life*

The fundamental fact of existence is that this trust in God, this faith, is the firm foundation under everything that makes life worth living.

Hebrews 11:1 MSG

Dear Heavenly Father,

How can I ever thank You for the gift of life? Nothing could be more valuable—or more of a miracle. I don't want to take this gift for granted. Help me recognize the beauty and opportunity found in even the most ordinary day. Then help me put my time on this earth to good use.

I want every single day to be an offering of thanks that I can gratefully return to You. I long to give You countless reasons to be joyful over the day You created me. May every breath I take be a wordless prayer of thanks and praise.

Amen.

Your life is a journey you must travel with a deep consciousness of God.

1 Peter 1:17 MSG

MY PERSONAL PRAYER

May you live all the days of your life.

Jonathan Swift

Dear Father:

___

___

___

___

___

___

___

Amen

Lord, help me to realize how brief my time on earth will be. Help me to know that I am here for but a moment more.

Psalm 39:4 TLB

In Him we live and move and have our being.

Acts 17:28 NKJV

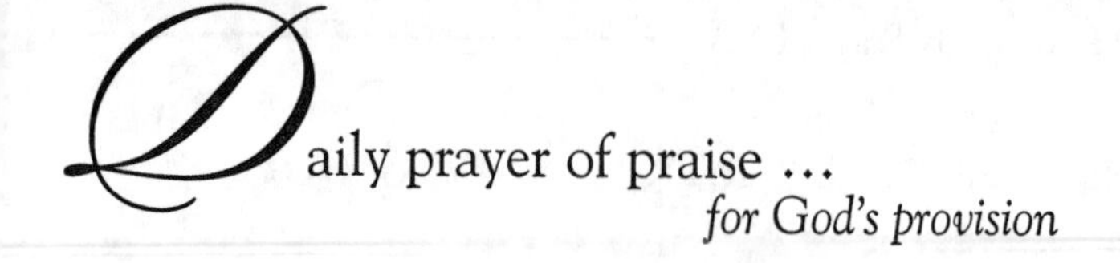

Daily prayer of praise …
for God's provision

I will send showers, showers of blessings,
which will come just when they are needed.
Ezekiel 34:26 NLT

Dear Heavenly Father,

You designed me to be dependent on You for so many things—the air I breathe, the food I eat, the abilities I need to make a living, the place I call home. Thank You for the many ways in which You go above and beyond providing for my basic needs. Countless times You've gone way above mere provision to overwhelm me with abundance.

Thank You for every blessing, both big and small. Help me to become more aware of the ways in which You take care of me, so my gratitude can continue to grow. Let my generosity grow right along with it, so I'll always be ready and willing to share with others what You've given to me.

Amen.

Give us the food we need for each day.
Matthew 6:11 NCV

MY PERSONAL PRAYER

God gives every bird its food, but he does not throw it into the nest.

Josiah G. Holland

Dear Father:

____

____

____

____

____

____

____

Amen

A devout life does bring wealth, but it's the rich simplicity of being yourself before God.

1 Timothy 6:6 MSG

Give me neither poverty nor riches!
Give me just enough to satisfy my needs.

Proverbs 30:8 NLT

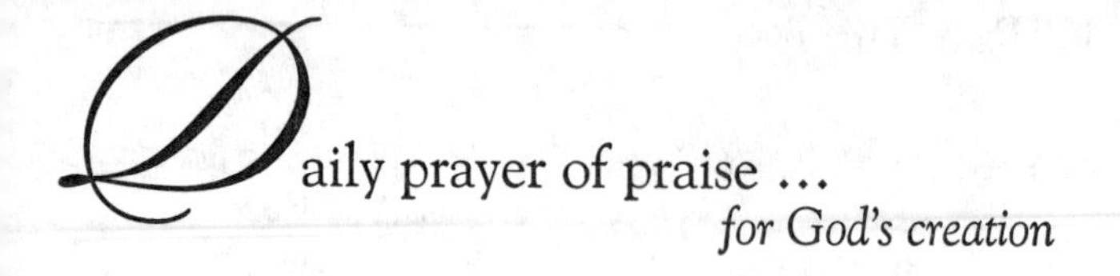

Daily prayer of praise …
for God's creation

O LORD, what a variety of things you have made! In wisdom you have made them all. The earth is full of your creatures.

Psalm 104:24 NLT

Dear Heavenly Father,

There is no artwork in any gallery on earth that can compare with what You've created. The world of plants and animals and people, of mountains and oceans and galaxies, is beyond anything I could ever imagine on my own—let alone create.

You alone are the one and only holy God, the Almighty Creator. Thank You for the beauty and variety that You've woven into the fabric of the world around me. Everywhere I look is filled with Your miracles. Everything You've made preaches a sermon about who You are and how much You care about the tiniest detail of my life. And I'm listening, Lord.

Amen.

From the time the world was created, people have seen the earth and sky and all that God made. They can clearly see his invisible qualities—his eternal power and divine nature.

Romans 1:20 NLT

MY PERSONAL PRAYER

Our Creator would never have made such lovely days and have given us the deep hearts to enjoy them unless we were meant to be immortal.

Nathaniel Hawthorne

Dear Father:

Amen

You don't need a telescope, a microscope, or a horoscope to realize the fullness of Christ, and the emptiness of the universe without him.

Colossians 2:9 MSG

Holy, holy, holy is the Lord of Hosts; the whole earth is filled with his glory.

Isaiah 6:3 TLB

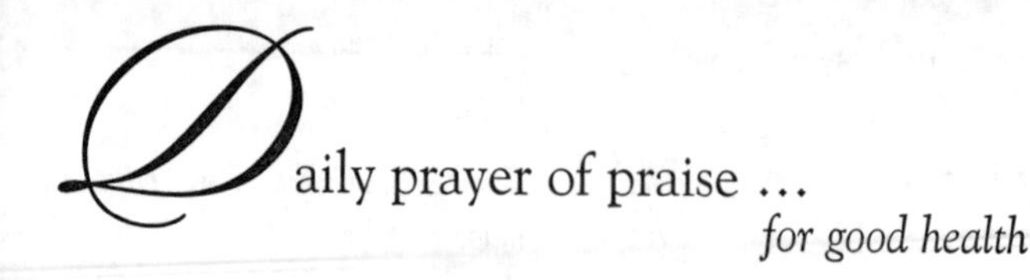

Daily prayer of praise ...
for good health

Keep my message in plain view at all times. Concentrate! Learn it by heart! Those who discover these words live, really live; body and soul, they're bursting with health.

Proverbs 4:21, 22 MSG

Dear Heavenly Father,

All too often, I only pray about my health when I'm sick. Forgive me. Every day that I feel great, every moment that my body is working well, is really cause for prayer, a reason for thanks.

Thank You for how intricately You wove me together in my mother's womb, for the time You took in making me—well, me! Thank You for all of the healthy days I've enjoyed in this life. I ask that You would increase my wisdom about how to take care of this wonderful miracle body You've given me. I don't ever want to take it for granted.

Amen.

Run to GOD! Run from evil! Your body will glow with health, your very bones will vibrate with life!

Proverbs 3:8 MSG

MY PERSONAL PRAYER

Look to your health; and if you have it, praise God.
Izaak Walton

Dear Father:

Amen

Lord, your discipline is good, for it leads to life and health.
Isaiah 38:16 NLT

A cheerful disposition is good for your health.
Proverbs 17:22 MSG

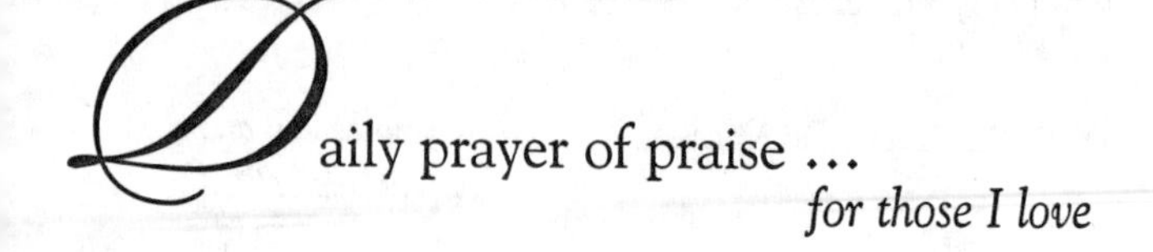

Daily prayer of praise ...
for those I love

These God-chosen lives all around—
what splendid friends they make!
Psalm 16:3 MSG

Dear Heavenly Father,

You have placed me in the middle of a circle of love. Thank You for my family and friends, for each and every wonderful person that You've brought into my life and heart. Help us to grow even closer together, showing the world what Your love looks like in action. Thank You for the unique way in which You made each one of these special people and for allowing our paths to cross here on earth.

Hold those I love close to Your heart, as well as to mine. Protect them. Guide them. Draw them ever closer into relationship with You.

Amen.

Thanking God over and over for you is not only a pleasure; it's a must.
2 Thessalonians 1:3 MSG

MY PERSONAL PRAYER

The heart does not need much space for its heaven nor many stars therein if only the star of love has arisen.

Jean Paul Richter

Dear Father:

Amen

Just as lotions and fragrance give sensual delight,
a sweet friendship refreshes the soul.
Proverbs 27:9 MSG

Let true lovers break out in praise,
sing out from wherever they're sitting.
Psalm 149:5 MSG

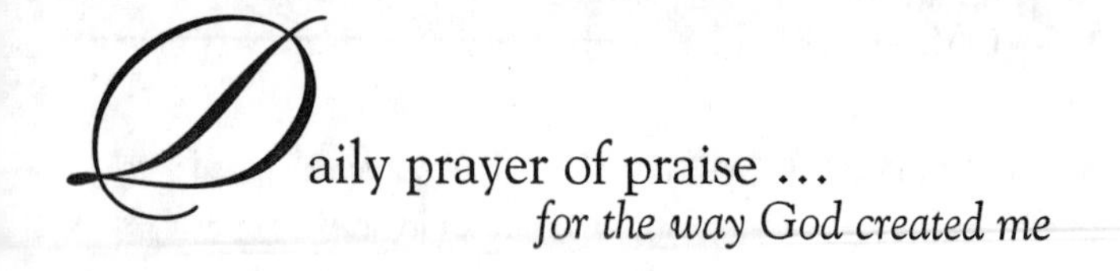

Daily prayer of praise ...
for the way God created me

I will praise You, for I am fearfully and wonderfully made; marvelous are Your works, and that my soul knows very well.

Psalm 139:14 NKJV

Dear Heavenly Father,

You know me inside and out. You fashioned me in the way You saw best, according to the purpose and plan You had for my unique, individual life. Thank You for the way You put me together—for both the joy of getting to use my strengths and abilities, as well as for my weaknesses. They're constant reminders of how much I need You, my Creator and Lord.

I know I don't always express my thanks to You in this area. When I compare myself with others, I often end up critiquing and criticizing Your creation, rather than thanking You for the way You designed me. Help me to spend more time praising You for Your work of love and wonder.

Amen.

Make a careful exploration of who you are and the work you have been given, and then sink yourself into that.

Galatians 6:4 MSG

MY PERSONAL PRAYER

If God wanted me to be otherwise, He would have created me to be otherwise.
Johann von Goethe

Dear Father:

____

____

____

____

____

____

____

Amen

Each of us is an original.
Galatians 5:26 MSG

You saw me before I was born. Every day of my life was recorded in your book. Every moment was laid out before a single day had passed.
Psalm 139:16 NLT

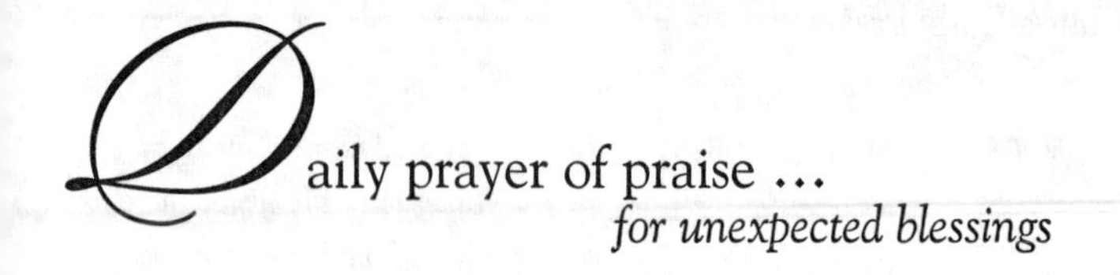

Daily prayer of praise ...
for unexpected blessings

Jesus said, "I came to give life—
life in all its fullness."
John 10:10 NCV

Dear Heavenly Father,

You've been so good to me, far beyond what I could ever deserve or imagine. Thank You for being a true Father in my life, for loving me in ways that deeply bless my heart. You know me and my heart so well!

Help me to be just as thankful for the little blessings that You send each day as for the ones that catch me by surprise. I truly am overwhelmed by both—Your big, obvious blessings and Your little everyday blessings.

I want to be more like You. I want to bless the lives of others, to share Your joy in real and practical ways. Please teach me!

Amen.

I will open up the windows of heaven for you and pour out a blessing so great you won't have room enough to take it in!
Malachi 3:10 TLB

MY PERSONAL PRAYER

Thou has given so much to me.
Give me one thing more—
a grateful heart.
George Herbert

Dear Father:

Amen

Happy indeed are those whose God is the LORD.
Psalm 144:15 NLT

Everyone will stand in awe, proclaiming the mighty acts of God, realizing all the amazing things he does.
Psalm 64:9 NLT

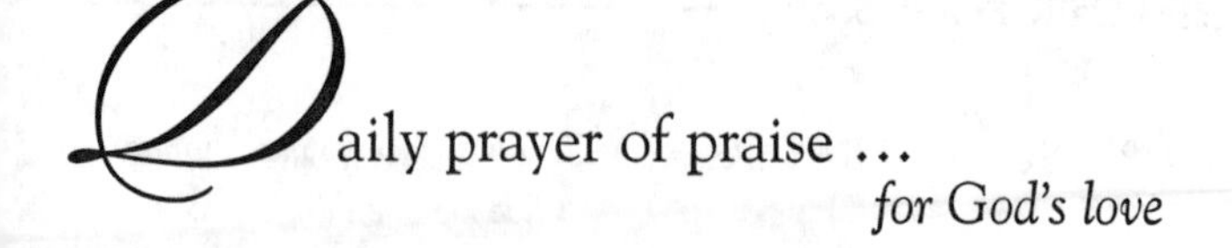

Daily prayer of praise ...
for God's love

Christ died for us while we were still sinners.
In this way God shows his great love for us.
Romans 5:8 NCV

Dear Heavenly Father,

Love is more than just a part of Your character. It's the foundation of everything You do, of everything You are. The depth of Your love has caused You more pain than I'll ever really be able to understand. Thank You for reaching out anyway, for taking the risk of loving people who could choose whether to turn their backs on You or love You in return.

And I do love You, Lord—deeper than words can express or time can record. This simple prayer seems so small in comparison to my love. But it's wholly Yours—a gift of love from me to You.

Amen.

If you are really wise, you'll think this over—
it's time you appreciated GOD's deep love.
Psalm 107:43 MSG

MY PERSONAL PRAYER

He loves each of us,
as if there were only one of us.
Saint Augustine

Dear Father:

Amen

God is love.
1 John 4:8 NKJV

Everything GOD does is right—the trademark on all his works is love.
Psalm 145:17 MSG

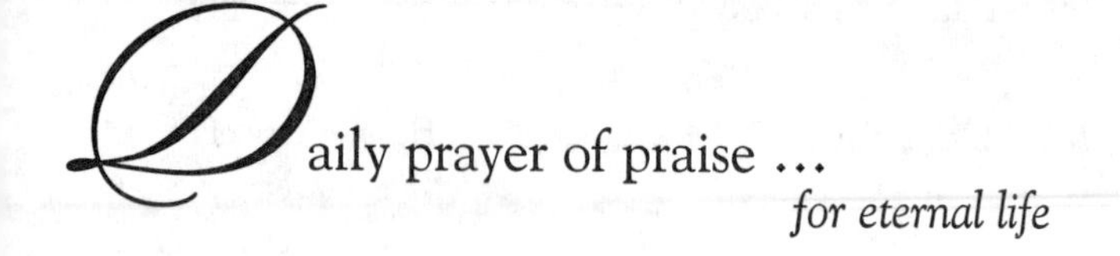

Daily prayer of praise ...
for eternal life

God gave his Son so that whoever believes in him may not be lost, but have eternal life.
John 3:16 NCV

Dear Heavenly Father,

Thanks to You, my life cannot be measured in minutes or days or years. Jesus' death on the cross built a bridge between me and You, between my life here on earth and eternity.

Thank You for that bridge, Lord. It's hard for me to imagine anything that doesn't have an end. But I don't have to imagine it—I will have the chance to experience it. And that thought fills my heart with joy.

Please help me live my days here on earth with eternity in mind. Help me hold onto that hope, even when death is near. Help me hold onto You today and forever.

Amen.

This is eternal life: that men can know you, the one true God, and that men can know Jesus Christ, the One you sent.
John 17:3 NCV

MY PERSONAL PRAYER

The created world is but a small parenthesis in eternity.
Sir Thomas Browne

Dear Father:

____

____

____

____

____

____

____

Amen

The troubles we see will soon be over, but the joys to come will last forever.
2 Corinthians 4:18 NLT

We who are still alive and remain on earth will be caught up in the clouds to meet the Lord in the air and remain with him forever.
1 Thessalonians 4:17 NLT

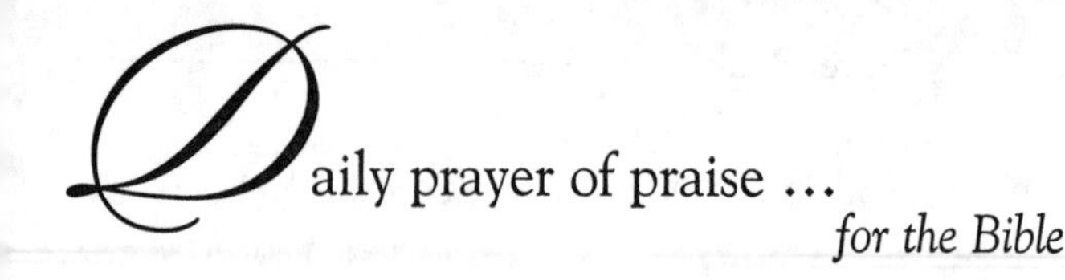

Daily prayer of praise ...
for the Bible

In simple humility, let our gardener,
God, landscape you with the Word,
making a salvation-garden of your life.
James 1:21 MSG

Dear Heavenly Father,

There are a lot of books in this world, but Yours is different. It constantly speaks to my heart in a way that mere literature or volumes of facts never could. Thank You for all of the people who took the time, and the risk, to share the message You entrusted to them. Every word that is written is filled with Your power, Your purpose, and Your love.

Please give me more of Your wisdom and perspective so that I can better understand what I read. Help me to become better acquainted with You by becoming better acquainted with Your Word. Use it to work miracles in my life, to make me more like You.

Amen.

The one who keeps God's word is the person in whom we see God's mature love.
1 John 2:5 MSG

MY PERSONAL PRAYER

The Bible is a letter God has sent to us; prayer is a letter we send to him.

Matthew Henry

Dear Father:

Amen

All Scripture is inspired by God and is useful to teach us what is true and to make us realize what is wrong in our lives.

2 Timothy 3:16 NLT

The entirety of Your word is truth.

Psalm 119:160 NKJV

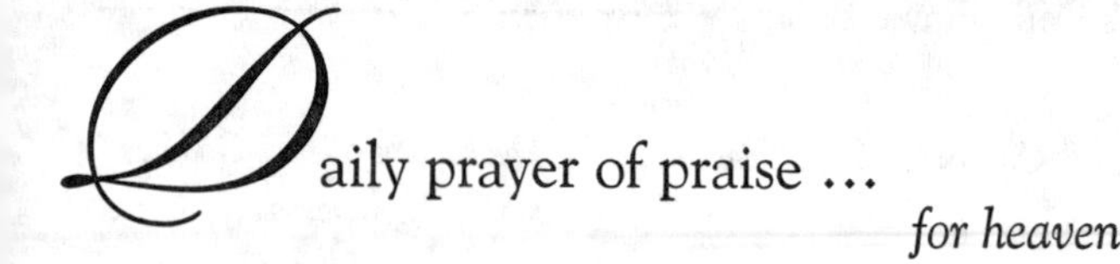

Daily prayer of praise ... *for heaven*

He puts a little of heaven in our hearts so that we'll never settle for less.
2 Corinthians 5:5 MSG

Dear Heavenly Father,

I know that my own mental images of heaven could never match up to what You have created—in the same way that I could never dream up such an incredible place as earth. But my heart dreams of heaven anyway. That's because I know that one day I'll be going home to a place where I truly belong. A place where I can hear Your voice and see Your smile. A place untouched by tears and bathed in love.

Prepare me for that place, Lord. I don't want to become so attached to this earth—no matter how wonderful it can be at times—that I lose sight of my true home. Make me homesick for You.

Amen.

Jesus said, "There are many rooms in my Father's home, and I am going to prepare a place for you."
John 14:2 NLT

MY PERSONAL PRAYER

We talk about heaven being so far away. It is within speaking distance of those who belong there.
Dwight L. Moody

Dear Father:

____

____

____

____

____

____

____

Amen

When we die and leave these bodies—we will have a home in heaven, an eternal body made for us by God himself and not by human hands.
2 Corinthians 5:1 NLT

Let heaven fill your thoughts.
Colossians 3:2 NLT

Topical Reference Index

The simple heart that freely asks in love, obtains.

John Greenleaf Whittier

For additions, deletions, corrections,
or clarifications in future editions of this text,
please contact Paul Shepherd, Senior Acquisitions
and Development Editor for Elm Hill Books.
Email pshepherd@elmhillbooks.com.

Additional copies of this book and other titles from ELM HILL BOOKS are available from your local bookstore.

Other titles in this series:

Life's Daily Prayer Book for Women
Life's Daily Prayer Book for Teachers